JIM & J

FOREWORD BY ED HINDSON
SPECIAL APPENDIX BY CARL BAUGH

SEARCH
THE SCRIPTURES
FOR YOURSELF

 21stCENTURY
P R E S S
READING YOU LOUD AND CLEAR.

SEARCH THE SCRIPTURES
FOR YOURSELF

Copyright © 2012 by James O. Combs and Geraldine Marquis-Combs

Published by 21st Century Press
Springfield, Missouri U.S.A.
Printed in U.S.A.

21st Century Press is an evangelical Christian publisher dedicated to serving the
local church with purpose books. We believe God's vision for 21st Century Press is
to provide church leaders with biblical, user-friendly materials that will help them
evangelize, disciple and minister to children, youth and families.

It is our prayer that this book will help you discover biblical truth for your own life
and help you meet the needs of others. May God richly bless you.

Unless otherwise noted, Scripture quotations in this text are taken from the King
James Version.

   21st Century Press
   2131 W. Republic Rd.
   PMB 41
   Springfield, MO 65807
   800-658-0284

ISBN: 978-0-9827616-3-2

Cover: Lee Fredrickson
Book Design: Terry White
Visit our website at: www.21stcenturypress.com

2131 W. Republic Rd., PMB 41.
Springfield, MO 65807
lee@21stcenturypress.com

DEDICATION

Shirley Wisner

Walter L. Wilson

David Wisner

Wade Ramsey

On the 80th Anniversary, 2012,
this volume is dedicated
to the memory of
President Walter L. Wilson,
prime founder of
Kansas City Bible College, 1932,
now Calvary Bible College,
and to his co-workers from 1932,
Shirley Wisner,
David Wisner,
Luella H. Gorden,
and Wade K. Ramsey (from 1938).

Luella Gorden

Walter L. Wilson

B orn in 1881 and born again in 1896 just before Christmas, Walter L. Wilson was destined to live a unique life and faithfully preach the Gospel, teach the Word and win souls for 71 years.

Although he was conscientious as a growing lad (although he had a mischievous streak) and attended church frequently, he did not actually receive Christ as his Saviour until he was fifteen. He and his mother attended a tent meeting at 9th and Agnes in Kansas City. Evangelist John Moffat preached from Romans 4:5: "But to him that worketh not, but believeth on him that justifieth the ungodly, his faith is reckoned for righteousness."

This ran counter to his concept. After four nights and four messages, 15-year-old Walter began considering the truth of salvation by grace alone, but continued to attend a church where the simple Gospel was combined with works.

Just before Christmas in 1896, he again attended another series of evangelistic services. While walking home that evening, he pondered the simplicity of John 3:16. As he was under conviction by the Holy Spirit, he remembered Colossians 2:14: "Blotting out the handwriting that was against us, which was contrary to us, and took it out of the way, nailing it to his cross." Pausing and sitting on a bench in front of a saloon, he prayed, receiving Christ, and knew that his sins were blotted out and that he was saved.

At the age of 17, he and a consecrated young friend preached on the corner of 12th and Grand in Kansas City. Thus began his long ministry for Christ.

Upon graduation from high school in 1899, he enrolled in the University Medical College in Kansas City and also studied at Northwestern University Medical College in Chicago, receiving his medical license in 1904.

Walter L. Wilson became a man of three professions – the ministry (his main calling), the practice of medicine and the time-honored profession of tent making. Like Paul, a skilled tentmaker, Dr. Wilson operated a successful business owned by the father of Marion Baker, his wife. The business involved manufacturing and sales. Walter sold huge canvas tents to Buffalo Bill Cody for his popular Wild West horse shows, to Ringling Brothers Circus and to Christian organizations for tent meetings and encampments. He sold tens of thousands of small waterproof tents to the United States Army for use in World War I.

In the mid 1920s, he was an early pioneer in Christian programming on the radio, having a popular half-hour broadcast throughout the Midwest. Later, he had a breakfast hour broadcast 6 days a week on WDAF. His radio ministry ended in 1938 when Dr. and Mrs. Wilson took a prolonged trip to Europe.

In 1920, the Central Bible Hall (Church) was formed with Walter L. Wilson as a major leader. Eventually, he was recognized as the pastor and served until retirement in 1961.

He authored 27 published books and booklets during his long ministry.

The College Begins

In 1932, Dr. Wilson with David Bulkley, superintendent of City Union Mission and Pastor R. Fuller Jaudon of the Tabernacle Baptist Church founded Kansas City Bible Institute (later College) with encouragement from C. J. Rolls, a great Bible teacher and scholar from Australia, who was in America conducting Bible conferences. Dr. Wilson, then 51, was named president.

During the early days, the fledgling school acquired an old 34-room mansion on Gladstone for a couple of years. From 1934 until 1945, classes were held in rented facilities in downtown Kansas City office buildings.

In 1945, the 75th and State Line Road campus was purchased for $45,000 which included three acres and three large buildings, including a dormitory and a gymnasium with adjoining rooms for classes. A beautiful 1900 vintage three-story mansion with a full basement provided office space, classrooms, dining hall and kitchen facilities, plus spacious rooms for faculty residence and a dozen bedrooms on the 3rd (attic) floor. Dr. Wilson was then 65 years old and was a much-sought-after conference speaker in churches and other colleges. The college continued to grow in numbers and influence throughout the 40s and 50s.

After he retired from the presidency in 1954, he continued his soul-winning, writing, preaching and teaching ministry until he went to be with Christ in 1969 at age 88. He had finished his course after 71 years of ministry.

Acknowledgments
Drs. Marilyn and Fred Moody
Arlene and Lyle Rohr Smith
Rhonda Long

SEVEN WONDERS OF THE WORD

We have all heard of the Seven Wonders of the World that have fascinated mankind through the centuries. Yet, for those who will examine the evidence, the Scriptures should hold an equal fascination. The Bible also manifests Seven Wonders of the Word of God.

1. The Wonder of Its Formation
The marvelous manner in which the Scriptures grew from the first 5 books of Moses to include all 39 books of the Old Testament and then the addition of the 27 books of the New Testament in the first century of our era is one of the greatest mysteries of the ages.

2. The Wonder of Its Unity
The Bible is a complete library composed of 66 books, written by 44 different authors over a period of 1,600 years. The authors came from different backgrounds, including kings of Israel, warriors, shepherds, poets, a physician and fishermen. However, the Bible is the most unified book in the world, containing a progressive revelation of the message of God without any real contradictions.

3. The Wonder of Its Age
The Bible is without doubt the oldest and most ancient book in the world, beginning with its first section of five books written by Moses 35 centuries ago.

4. The Wonder of Its Sales
Despite the fact that it is the oldest and most popular book in the world, its continuing sales year after year are the greatest wonder in the field of book publishing. Scholars have estimated that there are far more than two billion Bibles published throughout the globe.

5. The Wonder of Its Popularity
Every year the Bible is read by over a billion adults and young people representing every nation and class of people on the planet.

6. The Wonder of Its Language
The Scriptures were written in three languages: Hebrew, Aramaic, and Greek, by some 44 writers. Most of these writers were not well-educated, nor did most of them know each other. Yet, the wisest men of every age have acknowledged the Bible as the world's greatest literary masterpiece.

7. The Wonder of Its Preservation
There is no other book in history which has suffered more opposition, hatred, persecution, and outright burning. Yet, after thousands of years of opposition, the Bible has not only survived, it has triumphed over emperors, kings, and dictators who sought to silence its message of salvation through the blood of Jesus Christ.

-Grant Jeffrey

TABLE OF CONTENTS

by Dr. Ed Hindson

The authors began this challenging Bible study guide with a brief summery of the principles of biblical interpretation, including a listing of seven biblical dispensations, the eight covenants and the seven great judgments in the Holy Writings.

CHAPTER ONE
This beginning chapter is designed to set the mood and course for truly spiritual study. Five sections include: Approach Bible study carefully and prayerfully; Ask the Holy Spirit to teach you; Assign time to study; Analyze the Word; and Appreciate the Word of God.

CHAPTER TWO
Listed and explained are 10 basic laws for Bible study and interpretation. These laws are not original, but are here refined and restated. This emphasizes that while the Bible is a mysterious book, it is basically literal in its meaning, but contains symbols that are explained in Scripture.

CHAPTER THREE
Listed with explanations of each use are 10 basic books for the serious student of the Bible. These include with recommendations: a concordance; a Bible dictionary; a Bible atlas; a topical Bible; a dictionary of types; a survey book; a one-volume commentary; a Bible doctrines compendium; a Bible prophecy text; and the New Treasury of Scripture Knowledge (an amazing book with every verse in the Bible listed with reference verses and expositions). Serious students can acquire this little library of helps over time. All of these can be read and understood by lay people or fledgling teachers or ministers.

CHAPTER FOUR
How to Study a Bible Book
Here is a program for examining each of the 66 books of the Bible with a curious and sanctified mind. Spiritual truth, devotional truth and fascinating facts can be assembled by this systematic program of single book study. Whether with Romans or Zechariah, this method is most helpful.

CHAPTER FIVE
How to Study a Bible Chapter
Each of the 1,189 chapters in the Bible may be examined and explained by using simple steps of careful analysis. Emphasis, as in all of this study, is on spiritual lessons and applications to the heart from the Word.

CHAPTER SIX
How to Study a Bible Verse
Again, with over 30,000 verses in the Bible, many may be examined with spiritual profit. Here are 8 approaches to the verse, revealing different facets of truth and wisdom shining forth from one jewel of Scripture, providing much wisdom and spiritual joy.

CHAPTER SEVEN
How to Study a Bible Word
There are literally hundreds of words to study, examining how they are used in Scripture and what benefit each word can bring to our souls and minds. Such words as *joy, rejoice, faith, overcome, must, suffering*, etc.

CHAPTER EIGHT
How to Study a Bible Topic
The reader is encouraged to use a *Thompson's Chain Reference Bible* and/or a *Nave's Topical Bible or Zondervan's Topical Bible* to ferret out hundreds of topics discussed in Scripture. The chapter focuses on studying a theme, studying by actions (walking, sitting, running, etc.), and studying by objects, both animate and inanimate (things like camels, horses, dogs or ravens . . . or tools, weapons, buildings, trees, almost anything). Every object in the Bible carries a message and a lesson.

CHAPTER NINE
How to Study Bible Types
This fascinating approach to divinely-endorsed symbolical and typical meanings of many things can open up vast vistas of truth. The Passover Lamb representing Christ; the history of Joseph, paralleling Christ's ministry; the typical meaning of the Red Sea, the Rock in the Wilderness, and the amazing truths in the Tabernacle can all convey much divinely-inspired wisdom to the heart and mind.

CHAPTER TEN
How to Study Bible Numbers
This is most intriguing, but does not strain the mind or wrest the Scriptures. There are

obvious special meanings to numbers, including ONE through TEN, and TWELVE, FORTY and SEVENTY. SEVEN is the most-used and most-significant in Scripture. This chapter helps the student understand God's use of these numbers, but avoids erroneous "numerology."

CHAPTER ELEVEN
Both fulfilled and unfulfilled prophecy can be a source of much spiritual truth. The focus is on consideration of prophecy as an evidence for divine inspiration, but warns against extremism, date setting or forcing a passage to mean something beyond what it says. There are a few paragraphs on the famous "Seventy weeks of Daniel (chapter 9)."

CHAPTER TWELVE
The reader is encouraged to look at Old Testament personalities and to learn from what they did, whether good or bad. New Testament personalities, such as the Twelve Apostles, Paul, Mary, the Mother of our Lord, and many others can be studied with much profit. Part of the chapter deals with studying the life of Christ.

CHAPTER THIRTEEN
A doctrine is one of the primary ideas or teachings of the Bible, particularly a fundamental and vital truth like the Virgin Birth of Christ, the Second Coming, or the Inspiration of the Scriptures. Readers are encouraged to consult their church's doctrinal statement or Confession of Faith. At least 30 and perhaps as many as a hundred major truths or themes in the Bible can be considered important doctrines. Reference books are suggested.

CHAPTER FOURTEEN
Most evangelicals see at least three dispensations: The Jewish and Legal Dispensation; the Christian or Grace Dispensation; and the Kingdom or Millennial Dispensation. A large number see seven dispensations in the study of the Word, but the first four appear in Genesis and are stages in early Biblical history. Extremist views are to be avoided since all the Bible is for believers, though some Scripture applies specifically to the Jews, others to Christians.

CHAPTER FIFTEEN
Another interesting study is showing how God made covenants, some unconditional and others conditional, with Adam, Noah, Abraham, Moses, Israel, David, etc. And there is a New Covenant, which is why we read The New Testament (Covenant).

CHAPTER SIXTEEN
Since there is much poetry in the Bible, it is important to understand how the

Hebrews expressed themselves in poetic form under the guidance of the Spirit. There are many songs and poems not always evident in English in the historical books and in the prophetic books. Job, Psalms, Proverbs, Ecclesiastes, the Song of Solomon and Lamentations are practically all poetic compositions. They all contain valuable spiritual truth to be discerned.

CHAPTER SEVENTEEN
How to Begin Simple Greek/Hebrew Word Studies
A series on Bible study would be incomplete without showing the reader how to use some simple tools to understand beautiful shades of meaning and aspects of truth which do not always appear in English or any other language except Hebrew and Greek. There are no great mysteries or unrevealed ideas in these languages, but valuable lessons can be drawn from simple studies by any Christian. This chapter shows how to do just that.

CHAPTER EIGHTEEN
How to Read the Scriptures
Here are some plans for reading through the Word of God with retention and understanding. Practical suggestions on where and how to read, plus plans for annual readings are outlined.

CHAPTER NINETEEN
How to Memorize the Scriptures
Not nearly as many people memorize the Word as in former years. This chapter suggests various plans and programs for truly "hiding the Word of God in the heart."

CHAPTER TWENTY
How to Mark Your Bible
Spiritual Christians almost always want to mark certain passages. This chapter illustrates how to connect words and ideas with lines, how to underline, and how to use a color code system if desired.

CHAPTER TWENTY-ONE
How to Practice What You Learn
Making the Bible a part of your life, obeying its commands, meditating in its truth and witnessing to others are stressed in this appropriate chapter.

CHAPTER TWENTY-TWO
How to Teach and Preach What You Learn
Concluding this helpful volume is a challenge to witness, share Bible truth with other believers, perhaps teach a class or lead a group, or even preach the Word, as a layperson or a full-fledged minister of the Gospel. How to prepare and present a lesson is included.

APPENDICES

The Names of the Trinity

For a deeper understanding of Who God is and what God does, the following Appendices compiled by Elmer Towns of Liberty University in Lynchburg, Virginia have been included for your edification.

A study guide for *Search the Scriptures for Yourself* has been prepared by Stephen Rost, BA, MA, MDIV, STD and can be downloaded at www.21stcenturypress.com.

These (Bereans) were more noble than those in Thessalonica, in that they received the word with all readiness of mind, and searched the scriptures daily, whether those things were so (Acts 17:11).

Search the scriptures; for in them ye think ye have eternal life: and they are they which testify of me (John 5:39).

SEARCH

Studying the Bible has been a lifelong passion of James O. Combs and Jeri Marquis-Combs. They are experts at helping ordinary people discover the extraordinary treasures of the inspired Scriptures. *Search the Scriptures for Yourself* will take you from just listening to others talk about the Bible to the point where you can research its truths for yourself. Don't wait for the "experts" to tell you what the Bible means. Discover the truth for yourself.

Every chapter in their new book is a practical guide to help study, interpret and understand the message of the Bible. Practical guidelines will point you to the best tools to help you dig out the truths in the books of the Bible. Studying the Scripture for yourself will equip you to examine the pages of Holy Scripture with confidence and assurance.

Jim and Jeri combine their expertise to provide the reader with a practical and positive approach to studying the fascinating details of the Bible. Their study includes key chapters and verses, important biblical topics, types, numbers, prophecies, doctrines, dispensations and covenants. They will also introduce you to the basics of Bible reading, marking, memorizing and practicing the truths of scripture in your own personal life.

This is the finest guide to basic Bible study I have ever seen. You will be amazed at what this will do for your personal study and the impact these truths will have on your personal life. Be prepared for a wonderful adventure in God's Word as you let the light of truth shine in your heart after each discovery.

Dr. Ed Hindson
Vice President
Liberty University

Blessed [is] the man that walketh not in the counsel of the ungodly, nor standeth in the way of sinners, nor sitteth in the seat of the scornful. But his delight [is] in the law of the LORD; and in his law doth he meditate day and night (Psalms 1:1,2).

The words of the LORD [are] pure words: [as] silver tried in a furnace of earth, purified seven times (Psalms 12:6).

Their line is gone out through all the earth, and their words to the end of the world. In them hath he set a tabernacle for the sun, (Psalms 19:4).

Thy word [is] a lamp unto my feet, and a light unto my path (Psalms 119:105).

Heaven and earth shall pass away: but my words shall not pass away (Mark 13:31).

But he said, Yea rather, blessed [are] they that hear the word of God, and keep it (Luke 11:28).

So then faith [cometh] by hearing, and hearing by the word of God (Romans 10:17).

Let the word of Christ dwell in you richly in all wisdom; teaching and admonishing one another in psalms and hymns and spiritual songs, singing with grace in your hearts to the Lord (Colossians 3:16).

All scripture [is] given by inspiration of God, and [is] profitable for doctrine, for reproof, for correction, for instruction in righteousness: That the man of God may be perfect, throughly furnished unto all good works (2 Timothy 3:16, 17).

The secret [things belong] unto the LORD our God: but those [things which are] revealed [belong] unto us and to our children for ever, that [we] may do all the words of this law (Deuteronomy 29:29).

For the prophecy came not in old time by the will of man: but holy men of God spake [as they were] moved by the Holy Ghost (2 Peter 1:21).

Behold, I come quickly: blessed [is] he that keepeth the sayings of the prophecy of this book (Revelation 22:7).

Introduction

RIGHTLY DIVIDING THE WORD OF TRUTH

*Study to show thyself approved unto God, a workman that needeth not
to be ashamed, rightly dividing the word of truth* (2 Timothy 2:15).

To rightly divide, to handle aright, to analyze correctly, to divide accurately, to view and interpret the Scriptures skillfully is the responsibility and privilege of the student of Sacred Scripture.

"'Rightly dividing' is one word in Greek *orthomounta*. It comes from *orthos* meaning 'straight' and *temno*, meaning 'cut.' So the verb *orthotomeo* (only used here in the New Testament) means to cut in a straight line. The Liddell-Scott-Jones Lexicon gives for this passage: 'teach aright.' It was used for cutting a straight furrow in a field or laying out a straight road. In the Septuagint it is used in the sense of 'direct, make straight, make plain.'

"N.J.D. White says, 'this use of the word suggests the metaphor passes from a general idea of workman to the particular motion of the minister as one who 'makes straight paths' for the feet of his people" (Ralph Earle).

It is this writer's judgment that "rightly divide" exactly carries the idea of cutting correctly, straightly, analytically the progressive revelation of the word and work and will of God as set forth in the Scriptures. Antidispensationalists do not share this view, but assert that those who see progressive eras or periods in God's dealings with the human race overstress the significance of this verse.

We concur with the concept that rightly dividing the Word necessitates a literalist approach to biblical teaching; that it involves understanding that there is an Old Covenant for Israel and a New Covenant for the

Church Age; that there is a distinction between Israel and New Testament Christians; that God has revealed Himself and dealt with the human race in successive dispensations or periods of time or "ages;" that it is important to understand that difference between Israel and the Christ, the reality of the angelic conflict or war between God and Satan, good and evil, the righteous and the wicked; the necessity of the New Birth and the consequent teaching of "two natures;" the certainty of future judgments (plural); and the distinction between the First and Second Advents, both prophesied in Old Testament Scriptures.

We disagree with those who would spiritualize away plain prophecies and promises made to Israel in the past and for the future, set forth in the Old Testament.

We disagree with those who would make merely figurative the future destiny of Israel or the millennial reign of Christ in power and glory on this earth.

We likewise do not subscribe to extremist positions that would result in that hyper-dispensationalism that would take such teachings as the Sermon on the Mount and say it has no bearing on this age, or those who would teach that only part of the New Testament is really for church-age believers. No thinking dispensationalist would subscribe to extremist teachings, reading out or reading into the Scriptures that which is not there.

WHAT IS HERMENEUTICS?

The name *hermeneutics* is derived from the Greek, which means to interpret or explain.

The proper object of hermeneutics is the sense or meaning of Sacred Scripture. It seeks to determine the writer's thought which he had in mind and expresses under definite circumstances.

By Biblical Hermeneutics we mean the art or science of those rules or principles to which the true sense of Scripture can be ascertained and explained.

The Bible has two kinds of senses: the **literal** and the **typical**. It is the only book in existence which possesses these two kinds of meanings. The literal sense is expressed immediately and directly by the words of the Sacred Text taken singly and collectively in sentences. It is what the words actually and directly convey.

The typical sense occurs when a thing, event or person is used to express something else or to foreshadow some greater truth.

There are three elements necessary for a true **primary** type:

First, there must be the real existence of the person, event or thing. In this manner the type differs from figures of speech, metaphors, allegories and parables which are illustrations which may or may not have any actual historical foundation.

Such comparisons, however, may be classified as **secondary** types and provide valuable lessons and spiritual applications, but should not be over-stressed or used to prove a doctrine. In fact, no doctrine can be based solely on a type. As an illustration of a secondary type, note Matthew 13 where Christ says, "The field is the world" in the context of that chapter. It does not follow that every time a "field" is mentioned in Scripture that it always typifies the world. Likewise, when the believer is compared to an "eagle" in Isaiah 40:31, it speaks of soaring above the circumstances, as one "waits on the Lord;" however, "eagles" may also signify other things, as in Daniel 7:4, where Nebuchadnezzar's kingdom is in view.

On the other hand, all Passover celebrations in the Old Testament consistently point to "Christ our Passover" (I Cor. 5:7). This is a primary type.

Second, there must be a similarity between the thing which is the type and the thing prefigured by the type. In other words, there should be some likeness between type and antitype. Thus, according to Hebrews 7, 8 and 9, Melchizedek is a type of the Eternal High Priest, Christ, as the Old Testament refers to him without any allusion to a father or mother or genealogy, although he undoubtedly had parents. There are many other similarities.

Third, it must be God's intention to prefigure. This divine intention must be manifested in some manner. Specifically, there should be some reference that designates a past event or person or thing as typical and suggestive of someone or something in the New Testament. For instance, Christ says Jonah is a type of the Resurrection of Christ (Matt. 12:39); the brazen serpent is a type of the crucifixion (John 3:14; Numbers 21:9); the Passover Lamb (Exodus 12:46) is a type of Christ, the Lamb of God (John 1:29,36); the passage of the Red Sea is a type of baptism (I Cor. 10:1-11); Hagar and Sarah are types of the Two Covenants (Gal. 4:22). There are many primary types.

Trying to make everything in the Old Testament a type or reading into the Scriptures some secret, cryptic meaning to be understood only by the spiritually elite with no basis in plain Scripture teaching is a path that leads to error and false doctrine.

There is, however, a third sense. It might be called the applied sense or the accommodated sense, often explained by the interpreter. It is a sort of extension that is applied to the mind of the sacred writer, and is neither directly nor indirectly intended specifically by the inspiring Holy Spirit. Hence, it cannot be used for theological proof.

It involves the application of principles and patterns that are applicable to believers, leading to edification.

These applications, while spiritual and helpful, have limitations. It must never be intimated that the application or the accommodation is the true meaning of a Scripture or a passage to the exclusion of the literal and obvious original significance. Applications must be made of all Scripture to people today, but within the framework of what was basically for Israel and of what is basically for the Church Age. Accommodations and applications must be used in a reverent manner with the aim of building up believers, as encouraged by Romans 15:4 and 1 Corinthians 10:6.

MAJOR CONCEPTS TO BE STUDIED

First, there are the Dispensations. At least three must be distinguished, if one does not subscribe (I do subscribe) to these Seven Dispensations as set forth by James R. Graves, the nineteenth-century Baptist expositor; C.I. Scofield and his predecessors and successors; Clarence Larkin, the chartist; and most present-day Dispensationalists, such as Tim LaHaye and Thomas Ice.

That there was an Old Testament (covenant) dispensation that related to Israel, but which also predicted the Messiah-Saviour, cannot be denied.

That there is a present age, different from the Old Testament period, is also incontrovertible.

That there is to be a future golden age, or millennium, predicted both in the Old Testament and in the New Testament, if literally and logically interpreted, is beyond a doubt. To nullify this concept necessitates spiritualizing away thousands of verses in Scripture and making Israel to mean the Church.

No Jewish expositor ever subscribed under any circumstances to this fantasy misinterpretation of prophecy.

As aforesaid, we subscribe to the basic Seven Dispensations:

1. **Dispensation of Innocence** (Adam and Eve, unfallen in the garden)(Genesis 1-2)

2. **Dispensation of Conscience** (from the Fall to the Flood)(Genesis 3-9)

3. **Dispensation of Human Government** (from The Flood to Abraham's call)(Genesis 9-11)

4. **Dispensation of Promise** (from Abraham's call—Genesis 12—to the Giving of the Law)(Genesis 12-Exodus 19-20)

5. **Dispensation of Law** (from Giving of the Law at Sinai to the Crucifixion)(Exodus 20-Matthew 27)

6. **Dispensation of Grace** (from the Crucifixion/Resurrection/ Ascension to the Second Advent)(John 19 through Acts 2-Titus 2:11-13)

7. **Dispensation of the Kingdom** (from the Glorious Appearing to the Great White Throne Judgment)(2 Thessalonians 1:7-10; Revelation 19-20

Understanding the dispensations is part of "rightly dividing the Word of Truth."

Second, there are the Covenants. Two are obvious, the Old and the New, but a close study of Scripture reveals that God has forged agreements with portions of humanity or individuals no less than eight times in Scripture.

Study therefore:

1. **The Edenic Covenant** (Genesis 1, 2)

2. **The Adamic Covenant** (Genesis 3:15)

3. The Noahic Covenant (Genesis 9:1)

4. The Abrahamic Covenant (Genesis 12:1; 15:8)

5. The Mosaic Covenant (Law) (Exodus 19:25)

6. The Land Covenant (Deuteronomy 30:3)

7. The Davidic Covenant (2 Samuel 7:16)

8. The New Covenant (Hebrews 8:8)

Third, the Angelic Conflict. This involves the rivalry and war between God and Satan, good and evil, divine angels and fallen angels (also demons), sin and salvation, and the flesh and spirit.

These contrasts are evident throughout Sacred Scripture, from Genesis 3 through Revelation 20.

Fourth, the New Birth and the Consequent Two Natures. To be right with God requires the New Birth (John 3, etc.) and a "born again" person has two natures, the old Adamic nature, still prone to sin; and the new "regenerated nature," indwelt by the Holy Spirit. Study Romans 6-8; Galatians 5 and 6; and many other Scriptures.

Fifth, the Judgments. Rather than one single future judgment, the Scriptures indicate a "judgment seat of Christ" for believers and Great White Throne Judgment for unbelievers. (2 Cor. 5:10 and Revelation 20:11-15).

It is clear that there are at least SEVEN principal judgments:

1. The Judgment of Believers' Sins at the Cross (John 12:31)

2. The Judgment of Self Regularly by the Believer (I Cor. 11:31; I John 1:9)

3. The Judgment Seat of Christ for Believers (2 Cor. 5:10)

4. The Judgment of the Nations at the Return of Christ (Matthew 25:31)

5. **The Judgment of Israel at the Return of Christ** (Ezek. 20:37)

6. **The Judgment of Angels after the Millennium** (Jude 6)

7. **The Judgment of the Wicked Dead** (Revelation 20:11-15)

Sixth, the Distinction Between the First and Second Advents.

It has been demonstrated that at least 125 various prophecies, specific details about Christ, were set forth in the Old Testament and fulfilled in the First Coming.

Some 329 special prophecies from both Testaments describe or particularize facts about the Second Coming.

Between these two events the Church Age, the Dispensation of Grace, runs its course, which appears to be drawing to a close.

By studying seriously and carefully the truths set forth in the book, avoiding extremism of any kind and reading the Bible for precisely what it says and teaches, the minister or layperson can "cut the straight lines," and see the Word of God in proper perspective as it relates to the history and destiny of mankind, the people of Israel and the people of God of this age.

To rightly divide the Word of Truth is to study that Word and to see the unfolding divine plan for the ages, clearly perceiving the ultimate outcome of all of human history and the final triumph of the King of Kings and Lord of Lords.

—Jim and Jeri Combs

A study guide for *Search the Scriptures for Yourself* has been prepared by Stephen Rost, BA, MA, MDIV, STD and can be downloaded at www.21stcenturypress.com.

The Word of God . . .
Study it carefully.
    Ponder it prayerfully.
        Deep in thy heart let its principles dwell.

Consider its mystery.
    Slight not its history.
        Thou canst not love it too fondly or well.
              –S. Franklin Logsdon

1

How to Approach Bible Study

There are three main methods of mastering the contents of the Bible. J. Frank Norris declared, "The first thing is to *read the Scriptures.* Second, *read the Scriptures!* Third, *read the Scriptures!!*"

Yes, it is absolutely essential to read the Word of God to master its contents. No matter how brilliant and powerful the preaching one hears, and no matter how profound the teaching a believer may hear, there is no substitute for personal Bible study.

READ THE SCRIPTURES

Approach Bible study carefully

Since the Word of God relates to every life situation and the Divine Author longs to illuminate the Scriptures, open them carefully and prayerfully, eager to learn, know and do the will of God. Ponder these two questions as you read and study:

First, what do I need to know for my head? What wisdom, what facts, what basic knowledge do I need both for absorption of Absolute Truth and for instruction applicable to my life? *"If any man lack wisdom, let him ask of God, who giveth to all men liberally and upbraideth not"* (James 1:5). Here is mental instruction.

Second, what do I need to instruct my heart? The fire of the Word of God will kindle a flame of devotional zeal in the heart as the Spirit uses it. *"Is not my word like as a fire?. . ."* (Jeremiah 23:29). Here is spiritual inspiration.

Therefore, study to educate the head and to inspire the heart. Each day we need both knowledge for the mind and food for the soul.

Ask the Spirit to teach you

Remember that the Holy Spirit is here to teach. Three words are important as we consider this area of truth: *revelation, inspiration,* and *illumination.*

Revelation is the divine act of communicating to man truth which otherwise could not be known. God's Word is therefore the *revelation* of truth from heaven.

Inspiration is the supernatural influence exerted on the sacred writers by the Spirit of God under which they wrote God's message with absolute trustworthiness.

Illumination is the enlightening ministry of the Spirit in enabling the reader to ascertain God's message.

Therefore, *revelation* comprehends the giving of truth. *Inspiration* embraces man under divine control receiving the truth. *Illumination* deals with man's understanding of revealed inspired truth.

> *"But the Comforter which is the Holy Ghost, whom the Father will send in my name, he shall teach you all things, and bring all things to your remembrance, whatsoever I have said unto you"* (John 14:26).

Only the Holy Spirit knows our capacity. A babe in Christ cannot grasp truths a more mature believer can understand. As you look to the Spirit, asking Him to be your instructor, He will illuminate the Word and make it a living, vital force in your heart and life.

Then, too, He knows and decides your future course. He will teach you things you will need in later life. A missionary in Zaire might need to know different things, unique emphases of truth, which a pastor in Texas would seldom use. But beware lest Satan get you to ride a hobbyhorse. A false teaching or an improper emphasis can always be discerned. If it is something other than the gospel itself which is being repeatedly emphasized and overstressed out of its proper context, or which must always be defended, then the danger of warping a truth and twisting it into a false teaching is apparent. Have a well-rounded knowledge of the Word. Look to the Spirit to guide you. Ask Him to do it. Expect Him to give you precious thoughts out of His heart, particularly applicable to your life and situation.

Assign time to study

Get alone with God. Do not try to study with others around or with the radio or television blaring. Get away from distractions. Do not generally sit by a window where the traffic or some outside occurrence might draw your mind from the things of God. Satan is a genius at distractions. He does not want you to study God's Word at all and will strive to deter you from it.

Study with concentration. Banish other thoughts about the bills, the yard, friends or business. Shut the windows of your mind and focus on God's Word.

Be systematic. Do not just open the Bible here and there and read a chapter. Some people confuse such hit-and-miss scanning of the Scriptures with Bible study. Decide what you are going to study. Follow a plan, either one that you originate or one laid out in a good book. You need not begin in Genesis. Generally speaking, beginner students should start in the New Testament.

Take time to look up marginal references and other passages suggested to your heart by the Spirit.

Analyze the Word

First, *read*. "Give attention to reading . . ." (1 Tim. 4:13). Read through the Bible once or twice a year. A helpful schedule is usually available at a Christian bookstore.

Since the Bible contains 1189 chapters, reading four chapters each day will enable you to cover the Bible in a year. Seven chapters read a day will carry you through the Bible in six months.

By reading just four chapters a day (15-30 minutes), the entire Bible can be completed in under ten months. With 260 chapters in the New Testament, it can be read in a little over two months. The authors recommend reading the New Testament in January and February, then the entire Old Testament and New Testament in the next 10 months, thus reading twice through the New Testament. It takes 70 hours and 40 minutes to read the entire Bible at a normal oral reading rate. A fast reader could probably read through the whole Bible in half that time, not aloud. It takes 52 hours and 20 minutes to read the Old Testament orally. It requires 18 hours and 20 minutes to read the New Testament.

In the Old Testament, the Psalms require the longest time to read: 4 hours and 28 minutes. In the New Testament, the Gospel of Luke takes 2 hours and 43 minutes to read orally. Silent reading is much faster.

When you consider that there are 168 hours in one week, 70 hours of Bible reading in one year is precious little, compared with more than 400 hours a year most of us spend eating for physical nourishment.

As you read, use markers to indicate the pages and chapters where you should next begin.

Second, *study*. "Study to show thyself approved unto God . . ." (2 Timothy 2:15). In the succeeding installments a multitude of ways to study will be presented.

Revelation comprehends the giving of truth. *Inspiration* embraces man under divine control receiving the truth. *Illumination* deals with man's understanding of revealed, inspired truth.

Third, *meditate*. "This book of the law . . . thou shalt meditate therein day and night." (Joshua 1:8). Cultivate the mental habit of identifying a verse of Scripture with everything you see, and thus learn to meditate in God's Word day and night. You will prosper. As you see a tree, think of Bible trees. Associate highways, hills, houses, lands, birds, rooms, everything you see, with something in the Word, mentioning it.

Fourth, *do* . . . "Now have I kept thy word." (Psalm 119:67). Apply to yourself every truth that you learn. Ask yourself, "How does this truth apply to me? How can I use it in my life?" As you obey the Word, you will become increasingly like our lovely Lord.

Fifth, *search*. "They searched the Scriptures daily whether these things were so" (Acts 17:11). Look for different things in the Word. Find out what the Bible teaches about everything. Compare Scripture with Scripture. Do not misinterpret a verse by taking it out of context like false cults do. When you learn something, share it with a friend. Thus you will be taking in and giving out the Word.

Sixth, *write it down*. Carry a notebook or a number of 3x5 cards or something on which to write down the truths you learn. As you think of something to look up, make a note of it and look it up when time permits. If the Lord gives you some precious thought, write it down. Keep a file of outlines, sentences, thoughts, and truths you can use on appropriate occasions. Always have a good ballpoint pen with you to use in marking your Bible and taking notes.

Appreciate the Word of God
It is the verbally-inspired, infallible, relevant and inerrant Word of God, truth in the absolute. "Great peace have they that love thy law."

Prayer to Echo

Teach me, O LORD, the way of thy statutes; and I shall keep it [unto] the end. Give me understanding, and I shall keep thy law; yea, I shall observe it with [my] whole heart. Make me to go in the path of thy commandments; for therein do I delight (Psalm 119:33-35).

INTERPRETING BIBLE PROPHECY

Prophecy is God's roadmap to show us where history is going. The Bible's predictions claim literal and specific fulfillments that verify that such prophecies are indeed from God. The key to interpreting Bible prophecy is in discerning what is literal and what is symbolic. Therefore, the best way to avoid confusion in the study of prophetic scripture is to follow these simple directions:

1. Interpret prophecy literally wherever possible. God meant what He said and said what He meant when He inspired "holy men of God [who] spake as they were moved by the Holy Ghost" (2 Pet. 1:21) to write the Bible. Consequently we can take the Bible literally most of the time. Where God intends for us to interpret symbolically, He makes it obvious. One of the reasons the book of Revelation is difficult for some people to understand is that they try to spiritualize the symbols used in the book. However, since many Old Testament prophecies have already been literally fulfilled, such as God turning water to blood (Ex. 4:9; 7:17-21), it should not be difficult to imagine that future prophetic events can and will be literally fulfilled at the appropriate time. Only when symbols or figures of speech make absolutely no literal sense, should anything but a literal interpretation be sought.

2. Prophecies concerning Israel and the Church should not be transposed. The promises of God to Israel to be fulfilled "in the latter days," particularly those concerning Israel's punishment during the Tribulation have absolutely nothing to do with the Church. The Bible gives specific promises for the Church that she will be raptured into heaven before the Tribulation (John 14:2-3; I Cor. 15:51-52; I Thess. 4:13-18).

3. For symbolic passages, compare Scripture with Scripture. The Bible is not contradictory. Even though written by numerous, divinely inspired men over a period of sixteen hundred years, it is supernaturally consistent in its use of terms. For example, the word "beast" is used forty-four times in Revelation and many other times in Scripture. Daniel explains that the word is symbolic of either a king or kingdom (see Dan. 7-8). By examining the contexts in Revelation and Daniel, you will find that "beast" has the same meaning in both books. Many other symbols used in Revelation are also taken directly from the Old Testament. These include "the tree of life" (Rev. 2:7; 22:2, 14), "the book of life" (Rev. 3:5ff.), and Babylon (Rev. 14:8ff.).

–Tim LaHaye

2

HOW TO INTERPRET THE BIBLE

Ten Basic Laws

These were more noble than those in Thessalonia, in that they received the word with all readiness of mind and searched the scriptures daily, whether those things were so (Acts 17:11).

Those who accept the Bible for what it says are under a curious attack today from those who are ready to lambaste "fundamentalists," "literalists," and "inerrantists," frequently attempting to downgrade the intelligence, integrity and scholarship of those who cling tenaciously to the doctrines of our forefathers.

Some assert that much leeway must be given to those who "interpret" the Bible in different ways.

This article will not presume to examine the scope and history of *hermeneutics*, which is the science of biblical interpretation, a study far too extensive for this journal, limited as it is in space and size.

However, for our readers and interested Bible students there will be set forth here *ten basic laws* for Bible interpretation, none original with this editor, but which as a whole constitute the fundamental principles through which the Word of God may be understood. They are compiled from many resources.

The Law of Actual Meaning
When the plain sense of Scripture makes common sense, seek no other sense; therefore take every word at its primary, ordinary, literal meaning,unless the immediate context, studied in the light of axiomatic and fundamental truths, indicates a figurative or symbolical meaning.

Corollary: The Bible means what it says and says what it means. It is to be understood literally except when obvious figures of speech (metaphors, similes, etc.) or indicated (in Scripture) types are used.

Corollary: This does not preclude careful study of original language Greek or Hebrew words for clarity of meaning.

These thoughts are adapted from the concise "Golden Rule of Bible Interpretation," popularized by David L. Cooper (Ph.D., University of Chicago), longtime president of the Biblical Research Society in Los Angeles and one of the great Messianic scholars of the century. His eight-volume study, known as the *Messianic Series*, is the classic work on Jesus as the Messiah prophesied in the Old Testament.

Cooper and all fundamentalists rightly understand that God means what He says and says what He means. If the Word of God says "Israel," it means descendants of Jacob in whatever era they may live, for instance. When "Israel" is used in a symbolical sense in the New Testament (a rarity), it in no wise nullifies the usual literal meaning of Israel as God's earthly chosen people.

Second and third-century commentators on the Old Testament began the practice of spiritualizing the Old Testament, applying specific literal promises to Israel to the New Testament Christians who are both Jews and Gentiles. Fanciful allegorizing of plain Scripture wording resulted in myriads of false conclusion and many erroneous doctrines.

While some things are "hard to be understood" (2 Peter 3:16), the basic factual, actual, literal meaning of a passage of Scripture is fundamental to any logical comprehension of Bible truth. Therefore, believe exactly what the Bible says.

The Law of Contextual Meaning

Every Scripture must be interpreted in its historical setting and in its grammatical context with attention to who is speaking, to whom the message is given, and under what actual conditions.

Corollary: Every verse should be considered in the context of its paragraph (periscope) and in the section or chapter where it appears, within the book or in the division of Scripture where it is recorded.

A text without a context may be a pretext. Many theological errors are based on a Scripture taken out of context. For instance, the Mormon religion has made much of "baptism by proxy," an idea based on I

Corinthians 15:29: "Else what shall they do which are baptized for the dead, if the dead rise not at all? Why are they then baptized for the dead?" Obviously, the context indicates that it would be futile to baptize new Christians to take the place of the departed believers if there is no resurrection of the dead and Christ is dead and unresurrected. This is the only verse in the Word where this illustration is used. Yet, depending on one verse and only one verse for support, and that taken out of context and blown out of all proportion, it has become the basis of a major Mormon doctrine.

Always look at the context in studying a verse. Who is the writer or speaker? Under what conditions did he speak?

Christ once said to Judas, "What thou doest, do quickly," knowing that Satan had entered into him and that his diabolical plan was in motion. If Satan has tempted us to stray from God's will, does Jesus' command apply to us? Are we to hurry on into sin? Certainly not. That was a specific and knowing directive to the betrayer, long anticipated by our Lord and applied to him and him alone.

When the plain sense of Scripture makes common sense, seek no other sense; therefore take every word at its primary, ordinary, literal meaning, unless the immediate context, studied in the light of axiomatic and fundamental truths, indicates a figurative or symbolical meaning.

Do you see how important it is to keep a statement in context?

Study to find out when the statement or teaching was given, to whom it was initially addressed, where it was to be applied, why was it expressed, and then see what practical lessons can be learned from it by way of *application of a principle and not interpretation of a doctrine.*

The Law of First Mention

We may expect the first mention of a subject or truth to forecast its treatment throughout the Scriptures.

Always begin at the beginning.

Since Genesis is the "seed-plot of the Bible," most beginnings occur here; however, there are other "beginnings" or first mentions throughout the Old Testament and some in the New Testament.

However God first begins to reveal and describe anything is an

indication as to how the concept will be expanded and explained throughout the Bible until the last mention.

For instance, study the Holy Spirit "moving" as in Genesis 1:2; Judges
13:25; 2 Peter 1:20-21. The last mention of the Holy Spirit is in
Revelation 22:17. Babel or Babylon is first mentioned in Genesis 11 with
the last mention in Revelation 18.

The Law of Full Mention

We may expect a full and complete treatment of every subject vitally
connected with basic doctrine and consecrated living in a major passage
or section of Scripture. God will sometimes reveal His full mind on one
subject in one passage of the Bible.

As examples, find the Decalogue, a summation of basic righteousness
under the law in Exodus 20. Vicarious sacrifice is explained in Isaiah 53.
Regeneration or the New Birth is found in John 3. Laws of the Kingdom
are in Matthew 5-7. God's love for the lost is demonstrated in Luke 15.
Faith is extolled in Hebrews 11. Love is glorified in I Corinthians 13. The
Resurrection is discussed in I Corinthians 15. Pentecost is explained in
Acts 2. Justification appears in Romans 3-5, and so on through the Word.

Often, there are "norm chapters" explaining major truths. Look for
them.

The Law of Progressive Mention

From the first mention of a subject to the last mention, there is a progress
of doctrine; yet the first and last mention indicate what is between. The
intermediate matter is found to be fitly joined together.

At this point, a concordance and a topical Bible such as Nave's or
Zondervan's can be most helpful. Usually there will be a long listing with
many direct quotations starting with the first mention and developing the
idea all through the Bible.

Notice carefully, too, what God emphasizes in the Word. The more a
subject is mentioned, the more significant it is in the mind and plan of
God. Ideas or subjects mentioned only once or twice may be helpful and
significant but should never be overstressed or warped out of the context.

Everything that God has to say on a truth is important, and taken
together, constitutes the revealed mind of God in that field.

The Law of Comparative Mention

To compare Scripture with Scripture is vital to understanding everything about a given truth; all occasions in Scripture where a subject is mentioned should be considered to arrive at the total truth.

Therefore, compare spiritual things with spiritual things, Scripture with Scripture. Parallel and complimentary passages are to be studied together for comparison, contrast and completeness.

Compare the indwelling Christ (Galatians 2:20) with the indwelling Word (Colossians 3:16), thus resulting in a full and effective Christian life.

Contrast Satan (meaning the adversary) and Christ the Advocate; Babylon and Jerusalem; Cain and Abel; first Adam and second Adam, truth and error, light and darkness, etc.

Study "works" in the Bible, using your concordance and topical Bible, discovering what are good works, dead works, wicked works, and so on.

The Law of Illustration

For most truths, God gives one classic illustration to carry the truth home to the heart and mind of the believer.

Job is a case in point for the edification of a suffering Christian. Abraham is a powerful illustration of faith. Elijah is the bold example of courage and discouragement.

A careful study of the Bible will reveal that there is one major illustration of punishment for nearly all the sins mentioned in the Bible.

The Law of Double Reference

The Law of Double Reference is the principle of associating similar ideas which are usually separated from one another by long periods of time, but may be blended into a single picture initially (the sufferings of Christ and the glory that should follow), and in which an historical past event may illustrate a future prophetic event.

Much care should be exercised in not pushing this vital principle too far with wild flights of imagination.

However, remember that the Old Testament prophets foresaw both the first coming of Christ and the second coming of Christ as future events, sometimes, however, so closely blended that they had difficulty comprehending the time gap between.

The prophets *"inquired and searched diligently, who prophesied of the grace that should come unto you; searching what or what manner of time the Spirit of Christ which was in them did signify when it testified beforehand the sufferings of Christ, and the glory that should follow"* (I Peter 1:10,11).

When Peter quoted from Joel on the day of Pentecost, saying *"This is that . . ."* referring to the outpouring of the Spirit, he continued to recount the horrendous events of the "day of the Lord" when the moon turns to blood, yet those events are yet future and for the apocalyptic times. Pentecost was the *partial fulfillment.* Prophesied events in their full range of effects will take place when there occurs the *final fulfillment.*

Often, the Old Testament prophets will speak of an impending judgment to occur in their times and while describing it will lap forward to the end of the age to give additional information which will only be fulfilled at that time.

Therefore, in studying Old Testament prophecies in particular, cautiously consider if historical events cast a prophetic shadow.

The Law of Spiritual Application

The timeless Word of God is filled with truths, principles and ideas that were originally relevant to other ages and dispensations. These may be applied to people today since *"whatsoever was written aforetime was written for our learning that we through patience and comfort of the Scriptures might have hope"* (Romans 15:4).

The Law of the Master Key

Christ Himself is the Master Key to understanding Scripture, for He is the Supreme subject in fact, symbol, history and prophecy for all the Word of God; therefore expect to find Him in all Scripture.

Look for the Living Word in the Written Word. He is to be found in Old Testament prophecies and types. He is suggested in names and comparisons. He is greater than Abraham. He is the Second Adam. He is the Ark of our Salvation, more wondrous than Noah's ancient barge, Who can bring us across the waters of judgment to our safe and eternal heaven on yonder distant shore.

All of the Tabernacle, that awesome tent of colors and small furnishings of wood and gold, typified and symbolized our wonderful Savior. The fact that the New Testament explains the tabernacle as a type of Christ, as we find in Hebrews, does not for one moment nullify the historical fact of the literal tabernacle as the center of ancient Israelite worship.

Ask the Spirit of God to give you insight and understanding as you follow these ten basic laws for understanding and interpreting the Word of God.

> *Study to show thyself approved unto God, a workman that needeth not to be ashamed, rightly dividing the Word of Truth* (2 Timothy 2:15).

These concepts have been drawn from the writings of David L. Cooper, Arthur T. Pierson, James R. Graves and many others who approach the Bible logically, literally and intelligently to see what it specifically says and what it stresses and how it applies truth to the human need.

Master these ten laws and be preserved from drifting into error.

Til I come, give attendance to reading, to exhortation, to doctrine (I Timothy 4:13).

Recommended Study Bibles

The following list of available study Bibles that are recommended may initially seem overwhelming, but you as a reader of the Word of God and student may have a special interest in certain approaches. Therefore, shop in a good Christian bookstore and consider what appeals to you.

It is our suggestion that over the years you procure one new Bible a year and read through it, using a set of colored marking pencils you find at the store.

If you are a lay teacher, a college student interested in the Word, or a minister building a personal library, then we suggest that you collect most of the books we have cited in these pages. Shop in bookstores (both new books or used), or on the Internet, or from the specialized book distributors, including authors and small publishing houses directly.

CLASSIC STUDY BIBLES

The Scofield Reference Bible
C. I. Scofield, Editor, Oxford University Press, New York

The Thompson Chain Reference Bible
Frank Charles Thompson, Copiler and Editor, B. B. Kirkbride Co., Indianapolis

The Dake's Annotated Reference Bible
Finis Jennings Dake, Editor, Dake Publishing Inc., Lawrenceville, Georgia

GENERAL USAGE STUDY BIBLES

The MacArthur Study Bible
John MacArthur, Editor, Thomas Nelson Bibles, A Division of Thomas Nelson Inc., Nashville, Tennessee

Ryrie Study Bible
Tyndale House, Carol Stream, Illinios

The King James Study Bible
Thomas Nelson Publishing, Nashville

ADVANCED STUDY BIBLES

Hebrew Greek Key Word Study Bibles
Spiros Zodiates and Warren Baker, Editors, AMG Publishers, Chattanooga, Tennessee

The Companion Bible
E. W. Bullinger and Sons, Limited, London England

The Archaeological Study Bible
Zondervan, Publishing House, Grand Rapids, Michigan

PROPHECY BIBLES

Tim LaHaye Prophecy Study Bible
Tim LaHaye, General Editor, Ed Hindson, Thomas Ice, James Combs, Associate Editors, Power Publishers, Tennessee

Grant Jeffrey's Prophecy Reference Study Bible, Zondervan

Prophecy Study Bible
John C. Hagee, Editor, Thomas Nelson Publishers, Nashville, Tennessee

OTHER UNIQUE BIBLES

The Chronological Bible, the *Sure Word Reference Bible* (with Complete Topical Study Edition and Greek Dictionary)

Kay Arthur's *International Inductive Study Bible*

The Life Application Study Bible
Harvest House Publishers

3

What to Use in Studying the Bible

Every serious student of the Word of God will need several basic tools for searching the Scriptures. "Of the making of many books there is no end," Solomon wrote three thousand years ago, and his words are more applicable today than ever before.

Trying to recommend just ten basic books for aiding the exploring adventurer who is delving into the Bible is not simple. A studious searcher who is familiar with Greek and Hebrew might select an entirely different list than one such as I (or perhaps you), whose limited knowledge of the Greek is helped by a *Berry's Interlinear* (English on one line, Greek on the other).

But for most laymen and a high percentage of growing biblical students, a basic ten here suggested will form a nucleus around which a larger library can be built.

Everybody needs:

A Concordance

The one in the back of some Bibles is useful for simple reference, of course, but it often does not contain the word for which you are looking. A concordance is an alphabetical listing of each word in the Bible with quotations and listings where they are found.

Cruden's is small enough and complete enough for use by laymen, most of whom will find Alexander Cruden's notes helpful. "This concordance is a library of instruction. It is a lexicon of explanations, a source of inspiration and knowledge" which is indispensable to the Bible student. "Over 200,000 references are within its pages." Try to get one with Alfred Jones' list of proper names in the back, "the meaning or signification of the words in their original languages."The authors generally use *Cruden's Concordance*.

Other concordances for the King James Version include *Strong's Exhaustive Concordance of the Bible*, which is so complete it lists all the "thens" and "theres." Also most useful, as it was to famous commentator G. Campbell Morgan, is a numbering system of the Hebrew and Greek words, showing what each word in English is in the original language and additional shades of meaning for them. This requires looking in the back of the book.

Young's Analytical Concordance, by Robert Young, is just as complete as *Strong's* and contains 311,000 references subdivided under the Hebrew and Greek originals with the literal meaning and pronunciation of each word. Often, one English word is used to translate several Greek words, each of which has a slightly different shade of meaning. No looking up numbers and listings in the back of the volume, as with *Strong's*, is necessary.

Someone has remarked, with tongue in cheek, that *Cruden's* is for the crude, *Strong's* is for the strong, and *Young's* is for the young. There is also a *Wiggam's Concordance* and a *Watkin's Concordance* (KJV), which may be for wiggly or walking people, respectively . . . there is a *Hazard's Concordance* for the 1901 American Standard Version, but its use may prove "hazardous." Various concordances are available in most Christian bookstores.

A Bible Dictionary

This volume contains an alphabetical listing of Bible persons, places, objects and subjects.

This writer likes *Unger's Bible Dictionary* by Merrill F. Unger (Moody Press, Chicago, Illinois), but *Zondervan's Pictorial Bible Dictionary* is the choice of others. There are several available, but these two are among the best. Unger is theologically sound, dispensational in approach, scholarly in content, and strongly conservative.

There are several recently published Bible dictionaries available in Christian bookstores.

A Bible Atlas

Many are available, the most complete of which is *Zondervan's Pictorial*

Bible Atlas, but we personally prefer the new updated *Baker's Bible Atlas* (Baker Book House, Grand Rapids, Michigan). Closely studying the maps, pictures and details of Bible-related lands will add to a full understanding of the geopolitical conditions of biblical times. Anyone who is going to the Middle East should buy, read and absorb a good Bible atlas prior to making the trip.

Several recently published Bible atlases contain updated maps and information. Select the one you think is most suitable.

A Topical Bible

This volume contains the great subjects or topics of the Bible, alphabetically arranged, listing in full Scriptures where that subject is discussed from Genesis to Revelation. Thus, any subject, like prayer, faith, arks, or locusts, can be studied quickly and simply. This is an invaluable aid to Bible teachers and preachers in preparing lessons on great biblical subjects.

We like the older work, *Nave's Topical Bible,* by Orville J. Nave, but others prefer *Zondervan's Topical Bible. Nave's* (Moody Press) contains more than 20,000 topics and over 100,000 references to Scripture. (*Nave's Topical Bible* is not only for knaves.)

Get a *Nave's Topical Bible.* Then use it!

A Dictionary of Types

There is only one to our knowledge, *Wilson's Dictionary of Bible Types*, by Walter Lewis Wilson (Wm. B. Eerdman's Grand Rapids, Michigan). Here is an orderly arrangement of thousands of Bible types, informative and enriching. The author includes similes, metaphors and other figurative expressions used throughout the Bible, and draws upon his rich scientific knowledge to emphasize spiritual, devotional lessons to be learned from their usage in sacred Scripture.

Anyone interested in types and symbols will be edified by this sane treatment of the subject, which never denies the basic literal interpretation of any passage, nor allegorizes away the plain sense of Scripture.

Order a *Wilson's Dictionary of Types* for your library. If it is not available in your favorite bookstore, try www.amazon.com.

A Bible Survey Book

With so many like *What the Bible is All About*, by Henrietta Mears, and James Gray's classic work, *Synthetic Bible Studies*, on the market, the serious student has a wide range of selections. But we prefer the rather extensive *Explore the Book*, by J. Sidlow Baxter, a thick, one-volume summation of all the books of the Bible with outlines, explanations, introductions and expositions written from a dispensational viewpoint.

Explore the Book (Zondervan Publishing House, Grand Rapids, Michigan) is a complete Bible course in itself, with study questions appended to each section. If you follow its study plan, it is easily equivalent to a college course in Bible survey.

A One-Volume Commentary

Many one-volume commentaries may be found in various bookstores. *Unger's Bible Handbook* is a good example (930 pages).

A Bible Doctrine Compendium

The most useful is *What the Faith is All About*, a study of the basic doctrines of Christianity by Elmer Towns. It is a simplified, logically arranged, systematic theology setting forth the basic doctrines of the Bible in 52 chapters (lessons), one on each subject.

No Bible-believing Christian who wants to understand biblical dogmatics should be without this helpful book suitable for considering one subject a week, either for personal edification, or teaching others during an entire year.

You may want to get a copy of your church's confession of faith or doctrinal statement and carefully read and review it.

A Bible Prophecy Text

Since one third of the Bible is prophetic in thrust, no dedicated student can neglect this field. *The Tim LaHaye Prophecy Study Bible* and other prophetic books by Tim LaHaye and various prophetic scholars should be the foundation for these studies. Find *All The Prophecies of the Bible* by Herbert Lockyer and use it.

A Bible Chart Book

In recent years, such writers as Slemming and Eadie have combined artwork and Bible knowledge to present in graphic form the contents of the Bible.

Study this book with a few reservations, but recognize that he was a master at his artistic craft and has been unsurpassed. His writing is clear and concise.

Those of liberal persuasion will be quick to scoff at using charts to grasp God's plan for the ages, but the value of visuals is indisputable.

Find a copy of *Dispensational Truth,* by Clarence Larkin, and study it well. Also, locate a copy of *Charting the End Times* by Tim Lahaye and Thomas Ice. Buy it.

Ten Basic Books for All Students

There you have it. Ten basic books for all students who seek to know the Word of God in depth. Many others could have been listed which are of equal value to those selected.

There are Bible encyclopedias, books on every doctrine, commentaries by the scores on nearly every book in the Bible, some complex and critical, and others simple, practical and devotional.

It will require time to build up an ever-increasing library of helpful volumes, but it will pay great dividends to have it at your disposal.

Every serious student of the Word of God will need several basic tools for searching the Scriptures. "Of the making of many books there is no end," Solomon wrote three thousand years ago, and his words are more applicable today than ever before.

One final word to preachers and teachers whose theological or linguistic expertise has carried them far along into exegetics, textual analysis and bibliological logarithms . . (whatever that might be) . . .

Learn all you can, but feed God's sheep and His lambs with truth they can grasp with ease as the Spirit illuminates their minds.

So when they had dined, Jesus saith to Simon Peter, Simon, [son] of Jonas, lovest thou me more than these? He saith unto him, Yea, Lord; thou knowest that I love thee. He saith unto him, Feed my lambs.

He saith to him again the second time, Simon, [son] of Jonas, lovest thou me? He saith unto him, Yea, Lord; thou knowest that I love thee. He saith unto him, Feed my sheep.

He saith unto him the third time, Simon, [son] of Jonas, lovest thou me? Peter was grieved because he said unto him the third time, Lovest thou me? And he said unto him, Lord, thou knowest all things; thou knowest that I love thee. Jesus saith unto him, Feed my sheep (John 21:15-17).

When sharing the truth of Sacred Scripture, remember to feed the young lambs as well as the sheep.

4

How to Study a Book of the Bible

Since there are 66 books in the Bible, here is a method by which each book, regardless of length, can be studied and understood. Henrietta Mears' book, *What the Bible is All About*, is arranged in 52 sections, with surveys of each book, suitable for a year-long study, one book a week.

An hour a day of personal Bible study using this valuable and profitable method of mastering the contents of each book will prove to be edifying, life transforming and inspirational.

Read the book

The more times a book is read, the more fruitful will be the study. Reading a book several times will enable the student to view the book as a whole, and thereby guard against interpretations that are out of context. If possible, read the book out loud at least once, or listen to it on a cassette tape. Reading the whole book in one sitting is most helpful, except for Psalms and Isaiah, which may prove a little too long for a continuous reading. All New Testament books can be read separately in not much more than an hour, even Luke, if you read right along and meditate on specific passages later.

Read each book with a view of getting the mind of God and the message of God through the writer, both to the people to whom the book was directed originally, and to your own mind and heart.

Study the background of the book

Your Bible dictionary will contain a complete presentation of the background of each book and the conditions under which it was written.

You will want to have a notebook handy, and probably a separate one for each Bible book.

You will want to write down in your notes:

- **The author of the book**
  Meditate on the author. See if he is mentioned elsewhere in the Bible. Look up those Scriptures where he may be mentioned in your concordance and in your Bible. What kind of man was he? Why did God choose a man like him to write that particular book? Always read and ask questions of the Lord and of your self. Think as you read.

- **The place of writing**
  Ask yourself, "Why was the book written there?" Look up the place in the Bible dictionary. Did the place have anything to do with what he said?

- **The time of writing**
  Ask yourself, "Was it written before or after Christ? How long did it take to write the book?" Some books, like Daniel and Jeremiah, were composed over a long period of time.

- **The occasion of writing**
  What conditions contemporary with the writer occasioned the Spirit of God to inspire the book in that time? For instance, Joel says a lot about insect plagues and draws lessons from them. Do conditions suggested in the book exist somewhere today?

- **The purpose of writing**
  Was it to turn people back to God, as in the case of many prophets? Was it to revive, restore, record, remind, inspire, inform, instruct? Write out specific purposes that were probably in the mind of the writer and in God's mind.

- **To whom was it written?**
  Was it addressed to an individual (such as Theophilus or Philemon)? Was it addressed to a group (such as a church)? Was it a general composition for all readers?

Search for great thoughts in the book

Every book has a major theme and a number of sub-themes or topics. Try to find the major thrust of the book. What is God really saying in this particular composition?

- **Find the great truths in the book**
  List them. Decide which is possibly the main theme. Meditate on it.

- **Find the words used most in the book**
  A concordance will be helpful in this pursuit. Try finding the words *believe, life,* and *eternal* in John's Gospel. Look for the words *abide* and *know* in I John. When you notice that an expression or word is used several times, underline it in each chapter. Then look up the word and find all the places it is used in the book by examining a concordance. Ask yourself, "Why does God use this word or these words so many times? How can this help me understand more about God?" Find the word *precious* in I and 2 Peter, for instance.

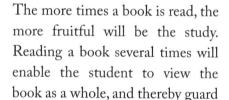

  The more times a book is read, the more fruitful will be the study. Reading a book several times will enable the student to view the book as a whole, and thereby guard against interpretations that are out of context.

- **Look for the characteristics of the book**
  Try to feel the mood of the writer. Notice the style. Is it simple? Is it complex? Is it forthright, or is there a possible figure of speech intended?

- **List the characters or personalities in each book**
  Is the author a main character, or does he scarcely mention himself? For example, Ezekiel is the main character in his book, and he speaks to 26 kinds of people using the expression, "*Ye shall know that I am the Lord,*" some 76 times.

(Incidentally, H.G. Wells, in his *History of the World*, uses a guessing expression, i.e. we think, we understand, it is assumed, we presume, it would seem, etc., some 726 times. The Apostle John, in his first short epistle, uses the word "know" 25 times.)

These things have I written unto you that believe on the name of the Son of God; that ye may know that ye have eternal life, and that ye may believe on the name of the Son of God (I John 5:13).

Analyze the book

First, as you read the book, try to see if there are obvious divisions. For instance, Paul usually uses the format of first presenting doctrines in the earlier chapters and then making practical applications in the latter chapters. Therefore, his books can simply be divided as: I. Doctrinal, and 2. Practical. Take Romans, in which the first 11 chapters are doctrinal, and the section from chapter 12 on is practical.

More complex divisions can often be made with no violence to Scripture.

Second, you can name each chapter.

Take the simple example of the Book of Ruth, with its four short chapters:

> Chapter One is Ruth Returning
> Chapter Two is Ruth Reaping
> Chapter Three is Ruth Resting
> Chapter Four is Ruth Rewarded.

Of course, it is not necessary to use alliteration for chapter names. Here is another simple series of titles, this time for Jonah:

> Chapter One is Jonah Straying
> Chapter Two is Jonah Praying
> Chapter Three is Jonah Preaching
> Chapter Four is Jonah Pouting

Be aware, however, that the chapter divisions are not necessarily inspired, but were made by Stephen Lancton, later Archbishop of Canterbury, in the 12th century.

Seek for the special characteristics of the book

As an illustration, consider Genesis. It contains seven beginnings, seven great men, seven great women, seven great events, and seven great types of Christ. Find them.

Also note what a book does not say. John omits the story of Christ's birth. Why? He only gives us 8 of the 37 miracles Christ is recorded as performing. Why?

Remember that Revelation is a book of the future, showing us the future of believers, the devil, the church, Israel, the earth, Christ, the unsaved . . .

List the lessons from the book that especially relate to our times and to our own hearts.

We are encouraging you to study the Word of God devotionally rather than from a purely analytical and critical standpoint. The Bible is a living Book, and its principles, teachings, ideas and lessons enable us to find truth and live victorious lives. Enjoy Him and His blessings to the fullest.

Ask yourself the question: How do these truths apply to me, my needs and my goals for victorious Christian living today?

Ask the Holy Spirit to guide you into all truths and teach you all things, bringing, *"all things to your remembrance."* (See John 14:16-18; 26; 16:7-15.)

*O*pen thou mine eyes,
that I may behold wondrous
things out of thy law
(Psalms 119:18).

As Tim LaHaye Suggests

We have already seen that reading is at the heart of all learning, and the best reading method is every day for 15 to 30 minutes. The same thing applies for a single chapter, except that you should read it over ten to twelve times before attempting an analysis. One thing you can do that will really make the chapter come to life is underline the verbs. The action of a passage is shown in its verbs, after underlining them, you can easily see the flow of a passage by going back and studying the verbs. Consider the following passage in Romans 6:11-13:

Likewise, you also, <u>reckon</u> yourselves to be dead indeed to sin, but <u>alive</u> to God in Jesus Christ our Lord. Therefore do not let sin <u>reign</u> in your mortal body, that you should <u>obey</u> it in its lusts. And <u>do not present</u> your members as instruments of uprighteousness to sin, but <u>present</u> yourselves to God as <u>being</u> alive from the dead, and your members as instruments of righteousness to God.

Excerpted from *How to Study the Bible for Yourself,* Harvest House Publishers

---

Deal bountifully with thy servant, [that] I may live, and keep thy word. Open thou mine eyes, that I may behold wondrous things out of thy law (Psalms 119:17, 18).

5

How to Study a Bible Chapter

There is an often told story of Stephen Lancton who in the 12th century during a cross-country trip, made the chapter divisions that have been continued ever since. Such medieval lore may or may not be true. Some have even suggested that he actually studied while astride his mount and sometimes made the divisions when the horse jolted the scholarly rider.

No one claims that these chapter divisions are "inspired" in the same sense as the original texts, but Lancton, who eventually became the Archbishop of Canterbury, deserves credit for a job well done. The verse divisions, by the way, were not made until some 600 years ago, and were popularized in the printed Bibles that rolled off the early printing presses of the 16th century.

Because many sermons, Sunday School lessons and Bible studies consist of a chapter exposition, in essence, this approach to the Scriptures is of prime importance. Follow these suggestions:

Read the chapter four times
This will enable you to have a mental concept of the overall content of the chapter, together with a growing sense of its major thrust and basic teachings. Read it out loud at least once.

Look up parallel passages
Take time to compare similar verses by looking in the margin where additional references are. By the way, use a Bible with a good list of marginal references and notes. Comparing Scripture with Scripture is part of Bible interpretation.

Check the date of events
Knowing the time when a passage was written lends historical perspective.

Name the chapter
Make up your own title. It can be a couple of words or a more lengthy designation, but generally, simplicity is advisable.

Here are a few examples:

Leviticus 13 can be called the "Leper Chapter," John 6 is the "Bread Chapter," I Corinthians 15, the "Resurrection Chapter," I Corinthians 13, the "Love Chapter," Matthew 5, the "Beatitude Chapter."

Use a sanctified imagination, your own creativity and good sense. If you like "catchy" titles, look in the chapter for something slightly unusual, and build a title from it.

For instance, Matthew 3 could be entitled "The Baptism of Christ." Or, looking at it closely and noting words and symbols, it can be called "Earth, Air, Fire and Water." John the Baptist preaches in the open air close to the *earth*, living off nature with a diet of locusts and wild honey. Descending like a dove through the *air* is the Holy Spirit, while baptism in *water* is contrasted with a baptism of *fire*.

Take time to compare similar verses by looking in the margin where additional references are. By the way, use a Bible with a good list of marginal references and notes. Comparing Scripture with Scripture is part of Bible interpretation.

Have two or three sheets of paper or a Bible study notebook at hand, always writing down ideas, thoughts and observations.

Outline the chapter
In some Bibles, paragraphic divisions are suggested with a little character called the pilcrow sign "¶" while other copies may actually have paragraphic divisions. Notice that several verses may discuss a particular subject. See if there are abrupt or subtle changes of subject from one verse to another. Examine the verses and mark divisions. Name each apparent section with a word, phrase or sentence, making each designation similar in grammatical order and design.

As an illustration, look at I Corinthians 13, the "Love Chapter." The first three verses compare love with other gifts and qualities, but stress:

The Spirituality of Love (1-3)

The following verses give us different aspects of love, which can be called:

The Spectrum of Love (4-7)

Finally, the chapter concludes with:

The Supremacy of Love (8-13)

Suit your outlining to your own talents and tastes.

Select a key verse in the chapter
This will be a matter of opinion and option. In John 3, you might select verse 3 or verse 16, either one of which conveys the main thrust of the chapter. Underline the verse, copy it in your notes, and if possible, memorize it.

Underline possible sermon texts
Even if you are neither a preacher nor a teacher, mark the verses you would enjoy hearing expounded.

Observe the words used most frequently
Underline these oft-repeated ideas. Study them.

In Romans 6, mark the word "dead" or "death." Also, notice the word "sin," which occurs in various senses in the passage.

The word, "Spirit" in Galatians 5 is most interesting; as it is also in Romans 8. "Faithful saying" is another key phrase in I and 2 Timothy.

List and study the persons in the chapter
Look them up in your Bible dictionary. Make some note or observation about each person whose name you find.

Study the lessons in the chapter
No claim to originality is made for these guidelines for pursuing truth. Write down the headings and list thoughts beneath each section.

- Look for the *teachings about Christ*. How many facts about Jesus are presented?

- Find *examples to follow*. What did persons do in the chapter that left a pattern to follow?

- Locate any *errors to avoid*. Were poor decisions or actions taken by any of the characters? Are there sins mentioned? List them. Define them. Decide to flee from them.

- Respond to *commands to obey*. Positive, imperative statements are expressions of the Lord's will and should be heeded.

- List *promises to claim*. Observe whether the promise is conditional or absolute. A conditional promise is one based on compliance with a biblical instruction which then results in a specific blessing. An absolute promise is one always applicable, regardless of circumstances. Compare 2 Chronicles 7:14, a conditional promise, with Matthew 28:20, an absolute promise.

- Seek *prayers to echo*. The Psalms and the epistles contain many prayers with requests adaptable to our needs. Not all chapters contain a prayer nor all of these seven avenues of spiritual research. There are 625 prayers in the Bible.

- Consider *principles to study*. Often there are many underlying spiritual principles suggested in a passage. Thoughtfully read the words and absorb the truths, listing any basic biblical principles that come to mind.

Look up any places or persons mentioned in the Bible dictionary.

Search for unusual and interesting things
Psalm 52:8 mentions olive trees. By consulting the concordance and Bible dictionary, you can learn that olives and olive trees are used in nine different ways in the Scripture, each with a spiritual lesson.

Apply what you learned to your own heart

After each period of study, decide on some courses of action or improvements you can make in your own life.

Study the difficulties

There are things "hard to be understood," requiring study and research in biblical resource books, and prayer to the Spirit for guidance. Become a well-versed student and sharer of the contents of the Word of God.

Though I speak with the tongues of men and of angels, and have not love, I am become [as] sounding brass, or a tinkling cymbal. And though I have [the gift of] prophecy, and understand all mysteries, and all knowledge; and though I have all faith, so that I could remove mountains, and have not love, I am nothing. And though I bestow all my goods to feed [the poor], and though I give my body to be burned, and have not love, it profiteth me nothing. Love suffereth long, [and] is kind; love envieth not; love vaunteth not itself, is not puffed up, Doth not behave itself unseemly, seeketh not her own, is not easily provoked, thinketh no evil; Rejoiceth not in iniquity, but rejoiceth in the truth; Beareth all things, believeth all things, hopeth all things, endureth all things. Love never faileth: but whether [there be] prophecies, they shall fail; whether [there be] tongues, they shall cease; whether [there be] knowledge, it shall vanish away. For we know in part, and we prophesy in part. But when that which is perfect is come, then that which is in part shall be done away. When I was a child, I spake as a child, I understood as a child, I thought as a child: but when I became a man, I put away childish things. For now we see through a glass, darkly; but then face to face: now I know in part; but then shall I know even as also I am known. And now abideth faith, hope, love, these three; but the greatest of these [is] love..(1 Corinthians 13).

Through God we shall do valiantly: for he [it is that] shall tread down our enemies (Psalms 60:12).

Through God we shall do valiantly: for he [it is that] shall tread down our enemies (Psalms 108:13).

Why was this verse repeated?

On two different occasions, David uses the exact same statement as an expression of faith under trying circumstances. The first occasion was the conclusion of a prayer of defeat. The second instance was in a prayer for victory. Whatever your situation may be, claim these promises, asking God for victories in your life.

6

HOW TO STUDY A BIBLE VERSE

One of the most fruitful and interesting methods of mining nuggets of truth from the Scriptures is the study of verses. With over 31,000 verses in the Bible, the possibilities are limitless. Every verse contains or suggests a vital message, even the lists of names in I Chronicles.

Read the verse several times
This fastens the content of the verse in the mind. Memorizing it will be of great benefit.

Look up any places or things mentioned in a Bible dictionary
As an example, look at Isaiah 40:16: *"And Lebanon is not sufficient to burn, nor the beasts thereof sufficient for a burnt offering."* The Bible dictionary tells us that Lebanon is some 6 miles wide and nearly 50 miles long. It will describe the beasts that are found on the mountain and even discuss the trees indigenous to the area. This will give you a greater conception of the magnitude of the message here, which is that no burnt offering, however large with ever so many animals, can really atone for sin. God is so great (as seen in the context) that the most immense sacrifice imaginable in Old Testament times would be completely insufficient. Contrast then God's provided offering on Calvary.

Ask why the message is given
Each verse meets a need. Ask yourself, and the Holy Spirit, just what it is that is taught here and why it is relevant now.

Notice to whom the message is directed
Every verse is written to some group, nation, person, etc.

Ask how the message is given

Is it a command? Is it an invitation? A question? A statement? If it is a command, it should be obeyed. If it is an invitation, there should be a response. If it is a question, there should be an answer. If it is a simple statement, it should convey or suggest a truth.

Observe the context of the verse

When you read a text, always read the preceding and succeeding verses, perhaps the entire chapter. It is a jewel in a setting. A text divorced from its context can lead to an erroneous interpretation.

Look at Matthew 11:28. It is an invitation. Why does Christ make it? In verse 27, He tells us that He has all things. If anyone needs rest, He has it. If someone needs strength, He has it. We can come to Him because He has whatever we need.

Ask thought-provoking questions about every part of the verse

Why? Where? When? How? Who? What? And Which? Practice having an inquisitive attitude about the mind of the Spirit.

Always write down your thoughts

Whatever insight God gives you, record it, or else, nine times out of ten, you will forget it. Make an outline of the verse, noticing its grammar. Use a concordance to look up other places where prominent words appear.

Let us look briefly at Galatians 5:22,23, "fruit of the Spirit."

Note that it is the fruit of the *Spirit*, not the fruit of the flesh, of education, of effort, or decision (we see what the Bible does not say, thereby learning). These graces will not be in the life unless the Holy Spirit controls.

It is *fruit*, singular, not *fruits*, plural. When the Holy Spirit produces this fruit in a surrendered life, the cluster grows together with these nine elements. Ask questions about each one.

LOVE. What kind of love? For God, for others? For the Lost? What is love? Where does it come from? How is it expressed?

JOY. When is this joy most evident? What is it? Why is it important?

PEACE. When is peace best manifested? What kinds of peace are mentioned in the Bible?

LONGSUFFERING. What does the word mean? With whom are we to exercise it?

GENTLENESS. Are we to handle people gently? If we jump down their throats, will we give them indigestion?

GOODNESS. How does goodness differ from righteousness?

FAITH. What is faith? What kind of faith is in view here? Is faithfulness included in the concept here?

MEEKNESS. Is meekness the same as weakness? What was said about Moses and meekness?

TEMPERANCE. Does this mean self-control? What are we to control? Consider that the first three are Godward; the second three, manward; the third three, selfward.

Think of it! If you spent just an hour a day (instead of watching television) studying the Scriptures in this manner, notebook at hand, in three or four years you could master much of the Word of God! Yet, there is always more to know!

Look up the meanings of the words in a regular dictionary and in a Bible word reference book, such as *Vine's New Testament Word Studies*, which gives some insight into the Greek shades of meaning. Meditate on each word, applying each element in a positive spiritual way to yourself first, to others second. Ask God to produce these qualities in your life.

Hope

A Positive Expectation Based on God's Promise

When hope is in the objective, that is, something set before us, it always refers to Christ's Coming for His saints.

1. "The Hope" (Col 1: 5).
   Christ Himself.
2. "Our Hope" (1 Tim. 1: 1).
   Common Heritage of Believers.
3. "This Hope" (1 John 3: 3).
   We shall be "like Him."
4. "Hope of the Gospel" (Col. 1: 23).
   Revealed by, and part of, the Gospel.
5. "Hope of Salvation" (1 Thes. 5: 8).
   Completion of Salvation.
6. "Hope of Righteousness" (Gal. 5: 5).
   Vindication of the Lord's own.
7. "Hope of Eternal Life" (Titus 1: 2; 3: 7).
   The blessedness of life eternal in the future.
8. "Hope of Our Calling" (Eph. 4: 4).
   What we shall have when Christ comes.
9. "Hope of His Calling" (Eph. 1: 18).
   What Christ will have.
10. "Hope of Glory" (Col. 1: 27).
    The excellence of His glorious manifestation.
11. "Living Hope" (1 Peter 1: 3, R.V.).
    The lastingness of His livingness.
12. "Blessed Hope" (Titus 2: 13).
    Present joy and lasting bliss.

7

How to Study a Bible Word

Believing in verbal inspiration (the words in the original languages were selected by the Holy Spirit moving through the minds of the writers), we understand that every word in the Sacred Text is vital and valuable.

While there is some overlap between studying a doctrine or a topic which may be expressed in a word, there are thousands of separate words worthy of thoughtful consideration.

Obtain basic tools for studying words

A concordance is indispensable, preferably a *Young's Analytical Concordance of the Bible* or a *Strong's Exhaustive Concordance of the Bible* since the Greek and Hebrew significance of differences in the words can be compared. Secure a good, extensive English dictionary.

Select a word for study

In the concordance, look up the places where the word appears and read the entire listing. Notice how the word may be used in a single book. Note "precious" in 1 and 2 Peter, "much more" in Romans 5, "joy" and "rejoice" in Philippians, and "overcome" in Revelation, as a few examples.

Follow some guidelines

In studying a word, find the first mention of it in the Bible. This will indicate how the word is used throughout the Scriptures.

In order to gain a comprehensive grasp of a word, study its use throughout the Bible. The Bible uses some words in a different sense than is given in the dictionary.

However, look up the word in an English dictionary to get the various meanings in common language. Write down a definition.

Next, find the word in the concordance and look at the Greek or Hebrew word, whether you are familiar with those languages or not. See what Young or Strong suggests as a definition, based on the particular Greek or Hebrew word used.

Take, for example, the word "power" in English. There are two Greek words translated as "power." One means authority, as it is used in the Great Commission, where Jesus says, "All power [authority] is given unto me in heaven and in earth. Go ye therefore . . ." (Matthew 28:18).

Believing in verbal inspiration (the words in the original were selected by the Holy Spirit moving through the minds of the writers), we understand that every word in the Sacred Text is vital and valuable.

The other Greek word means dynamic energy, like a dynamo. Hence, Christ says in Acts 1:8: "But ye shall receive power [dynamic], after that the Holy Ghost is come upon you: and ye shall be witnesses unto me both in Jerusalem, and in all Judea, and in Samaria, and unto the uttermost part of the earth."

Jesus has received "all power" . . . authority . . . therefore, He can promise "power" [dynamic energy] through the Holy Spirit.

Just a little simple research can open vistas of truth not evident from just a cursory reading of a passage or consideration of a word.

Ponder these examples

Take the word "forgiveness." A careful study of the word reveals that there are at least five kinds of forgiveness:

Judicial, as between a judge and a criminal, as in Ephesians 1:7.

Paternal, as between a father and a child, as in I John 1:9.

Fraternal, as between brethren. See Ephesians 4:32.

Social, as between neighbors. Study Matthew 5:23-25.

Ecclesiastical, as between a church and members. Study I Corinthians 3 and 5.

The word "must" in the gospel of John is very interesting. An outline for preaching or teaching can be easily prepared.

The must of worship (John 4:24).

The must of work (John 9:4).

The must of purpose (John 10:16).

The must of regeneration (John 3:7).

The must of sacrifice (John 3:14; 12:34).

The must of service (John 4:4).

The must of resurrection (John 20:9)

The must of increase (John 3:30).

They may be used in any order that seem logical and are consistent with the purpose of the lesson.

The word "must" speaks of the necessity and urgency of the truth declared. Another interesting study is to consider the 25 "verily verily" or the "amen amens" in John.

Additional helps for serious students

Especially useful for preachers and teachers are two books by 19th century Bible expositor, F.E. Marsh, both of which have been republished by Zondervan in recent years. They are *Five Hundred Bible Readings* and *1,000 Bible Outlines*. Marsh was a master sermon outliner and a specialist in the kind of word studies here suggested. Every preacher would profit from having these volumes, as would Sunday School teachers.

The use of *Vine's New Testament Greek Words* greatly enhances the consideration of many important words, since his solid, conservative exegesis goes beyond the elementary definitions in the recommended concordances.

Anyone who carefully examines the very words of Scripture will be the more convinced of the verbal inspiration of the Word of God.

> Anyone who carefully examines the very words of Scripture will be the more convinced of the verbal inspiration of the Word of God.

Studying Topics

The study of the Word of God can best be facilitated by a wise and constant use of a Concordance. Here you will find almost every word of the whole Bible arranged alphabetically, so that at any time the student may find the location of any passage that he may desire. By this means also, the student will discover that many statements are incorrectly quoted from the Bible. Sometimes quotations are made which are not found in the Bible in any form. This may be discovered by consulting your Concordance and looking for any of the prominent words used in that quotation.

By means of this Concordance the student may study any subject desired. For instance, you might wish to study the subject of trees. Find the word "tree" in the Concordance, and then notice every place where the word occurs, and what is the subject under consideration. You will find that the "oak tree" is usually mentioned in connection with death. The "fig tree" is usually connected with political Israel, etc.

If you wish to study the subject of "grace," or "horses," or of the "blood," or of the "coming of Christ," or of the "judgments," or any other subject, just find that word in your Concordance and look up the various Scriptures in which that word occurs. By this means you will become well acquainted with your Bible and with God's Truth.

If you hear a verse of Scripture quoted, and you do not know where it is found, seek the prominent word in the Concordance, follow down the Scriptures that are listed there, and you will find the verse that you desire to locate.

The Concordance is a library of instruction. It is a lexicon of explanation. It is a source of inspiration and knowledge which is indispensable to the Bible student. Permit me to encourage every student of the Word of God to own a copy of this wonderful and valuable book.

–Walter L. Wilson, M.D., L.H.D.

8

How to Study a Bible Topic

Indispensable to the pursuit of topical studies is a topical Bible, such as the previously recommended *Nave's Topical Bible* (Moody Press) or *Zondervan's Topical Bible*, both of which contain over 20,000 topics and subtopics and 100,000 references.

Useful, too, is a *Thompson Chain Reference Bible*, which has several thousand verses and references in the back of the volume, utilizing a marginal numerical system throughout all of the books of the Word to locate topics.

A small book with an introduction by R.A. Torrey, called *A Topical Textbook*, is also an aid in considering subjects of biblical significance.

Naturally, studying a word or a doctrine (separately considered in this series) will sometimes overlap, since such a word as JUSTIFICATION could be considered as a doctrine, a topic or a word.

Therefore, for present purposes, the consideration of topics will be organized under three sections. First, the consideration of a theme will be discussed. Then we shall ponder studying the Bible by actions, and then by objects.

How to study a theme
A theme, as we shall use the word, will designate a one-word topic, such as TRUTH (page 1324 in *Nave's*) in which a long list of Scripture references with some excerpted quotations is given, showing how the word is used and what it means. Studying all of these verses will enable the student to understand what the Spirit means when He uses the word in the Bible *"Study to show thyself approved unto God, a workman that needeth not to be ashamed, rightly dividing the Word of "TRUTH"* (2 Tim. 2:15).

. . . Or, a subject then can be considered, like COLORS (page 212-215 in *Nave's Topical Bible*).

There is a listing of various colors mentioned in the topical Bible, with many of the verses printed in full. Suggested symbolical (typical) meanings for the colors are offered in your topical Bible.

A soul-stirring, time-consuming program of edifying research would be most worthwhile if the student were to read through a topical Bible in a year, carefully meditating on each suggested theme. Several pages could be considered each day.

There are thousands of such themes, each one with many facets, like a skillfully-cut diamond, flashing new aspects of truths from every approach.

How to study by actions

There are many things done by great Bible characters which we should seek to repeat in our lives. Conversely, there are many mistakes we must avoid. Actions are an odd, but profitable, study.

Think of SITTING.

When you find a Bible character seated or about to sit, ask:

> Why was he sitting?
> Where was he sitting?
> When was he sitting?
> What was he sitting on?
> When did he get up?
> What lessons can I learn from his actions?

A concordance gives a great list of sittings, sats, and seats. Look them up. See Psalm 139:2; Hebrews 1:3; Matthew 26:64; Luke 2:46; Job 2:8 for starters.

Think of RUNNING.

Use the same questions previously listed, substituting RUNNING for SITTING. Research I Corinthians 9:24; Galatians 5:7; Philippians 2:16; I Peter 4:4 as examples.

Think of WEEPING.

Follow the same format in approaching the subject. Look up the word in the concordance, the occasions where weeping took place; then, with a sanctified imagination, seek answers to questions. Find out when and why Jesus wept.

Think of WALKING.
For starters, look up the seven times WALK or WALKING appears in the book of Ephesians.

Look through the concordance and through the Bible for others who walked with God, walked after sins, walked with others . . .

Think, what is "walking" in the biblical sense? Why does it say "walk" and not "run?" When do we "run?" Do we ever "crawl?" Notice what the Scriptures do not say, as well.

Think about some other actions and look them up, using the questioning approach. Remember doubles, opposites, contrasts, repetitions. They all have a purpose.

Continually have a spiritually-inquisitive mind! Even Rudyard Kipling once wrote:
I had me six serving men
Who taught me all I knew
Their names were What and Where and When
And How and Why and Who.

How to study by objects
There may be some overlap here with the study of types which will come up in a later discussion. But no mind, many objects that are not necessarily types can yield helpful spiritual truths for our daily lives.

Of course, there are two types of objects: animate and inanimate. Any object mentioned in the Bible is a fruitful source for lessons and applications for life. Trees, plants, clouds, mountains, buildings, temples, nails, tools, animals, flowers, birds, or just about anything that is discussed in the infallible Word of truth can be studied with practical, inspirational and personal profit.

- Settle on an object and look it up in the concordance. List its appearances and look up all the Scriptures, reading them carefully, always having a pencil handy to take notes.

- Look up the object in a Bible dictionary, a special book of listings (like *All the Animals of the Bible*, by Herbert Lockyer), and/or in a regular dictionary. Try to read about the object from an encyclopedia, if available.

- Seek to find what the Holy Spirit has in the object that will be a blessing to you.

Let us take a couple of examples and expand on them.

Jeremiah 46:4 says, *"Harness the horses."* God has some purpose for that beyond the immediate context. Think of how Christians are like horses. There is a need for teamwork with horses . . . the harnesses must fit . . . they are necessary . . . they are used for control . . . how does God harness us? Should we let Him be in the saddle and let Him use the reins of the Word to guide us . . .? Something must die before a harness can be secured, for it is made of animal skin . . . Who died to "harness" us? Harnesses enable us to work . . . Let every believer so seek to let God harness him and get him in the place of usefulness.

There are many things done by great Bible characters which we should seek to repeat in our lives. Conversely, there are many mistakes we must avoid. Actions are an odd, but profitable, study.

Jesus said, *"Consider the ravens . . ."* (Luke 12:24). If Jesus said to consider them, we ought to do it. Ravens are destructive, black, selfish . . . their offspring are like their parents . . . but their nature can be changed. See I Kings 17:4,6. It is absolutely contrary to nature for ravens to be interested in doing anything for others, as they did in the case of Elijah. What does all of this suggest to us?

A few other fascinating objects to study might be the lily of the valley, oak trees, fig trees, chickens, roosters, anything at all.

The more unusual the topic, the more interest will be stimulated and the greater the impression on an audience if you are teaching the Word.

The whole area of topical Bible study is simply inexhaustible. Remember, the Bible is supernaturally inspired and does not contain a superfluous word, a silly contradiction, or an unnecessary line. All Scripture is profitable. Make the study of topics part of your general biblical and spiritual education.

In-Depth Study

Look for Roswell D. Hitchcock's *A Complete Analysis of the Holy Bible* or *The Whole Bible Arranged in Subjects.* This publication contains every verse in the Bible, distributed according to its meaning and arranged with all other verses bearing on the same subject, fully indexed, furnishing simple and exhaustive means on what the Bible teaches on any one subject. Published by Assurance Publishers or Power Publishers at 912 S. Old McDonald Road, McDonald, Tennessee, 3735, under the title *Sure Word Reference Bible - Complete Topical Study Addition* (KJV).

It takes time, through prayer and God-given insight, to reach higher levels of spirituality, *"increasing in the knowledge of God"* (Col. 1:10).

How To Study Types

The student should first decide whether the word under consideration is used by the Spirit as a type. Not all objects are types. Care should be used in arriving at a conclusion on this matter lest one distort the Word of God and thus arrive at decisions which were never intended by the Lord.

A safe rule is to ascertain whether an object is said plainly to be a type. When Paul wrote in 1 Corinthians 10:4, "They drank of that spiritual rock . . . and that rock was Christ," we know that the rock in the wilderness was a true type of Christ.

When we read of the good and bad fish in Matthew 13:47, we know that these fish are types though the passage does not say so. The story is a parable intended to teach a lesson. It is needful therefore to learn just what they do represent and also what the net represents.

When we read of the "Red Sea" or "the Jordan," we know this to be a type just because it teaches so many very interesting and profitable lessons.

But even though we decide that an object is a type there still remains the problem of learning what it represents. Here, great care is needed. Let us ask, "What constitutes a type?" Let us seek an answer by a series of comparisons:

1. There is likeness of appearance as "clouds" and "dust." (Nahum 1:3)
2. There is likeness of action as "the leopard" and "Alexander the Great." (Dan. 7:6)
3. There is likeness of effect as "rain and snow" and "the Word of God." (Isa. 55:10)
4. There is likeness of relationship as "nurse" and "Paul." (I Thess. 2:7)
5. There is likeness of value as "gold" and "the Lord Jesus." (Isa. 13:12)
6. There is likeness of position as "head" and "Israel." (Deut. 28:13)
7. There is likeness of character as "the spider" and "the sinner." (Prov. 30:28)

–Walter L. Wilson, M.D., L.H.D.

HOW TO STUDY BIBLE TYPES

The serious Bible student should seek to avoid two extremes in this specialized field of biblical research known as *Typology*. First, completely ignoring this fascinating authentic approach to better understanding of the Word of God is a common practice of liberal theologians who claim such symbolism is both imaginary and useless. On the other hand, the mystically-minded scholar may search for hidden meanings in the simplest of biblical narratives where no typical teaching is in view.

Again, balance is vital.

As for biblical interpretation, an early mention of technique is found in Nehemiah 8:8: *"So they read in the book of the law of God distinctly, and gave the sense, and caused them to understand the reading."*

Not only does this verse provide basic guidelines for all biblical exposition, but it stresses the importance of giving "the sense."

Now, there are no more than three basic "senses" in any portion of Scripture, although there is the possibility of an implied or theological sense that can be based on the general and total teaching of the Bible. That, however, is more in the realm of biblical philosophy and systematic theology than in the area of Bible exposition.

These basic senses are: the literal which is immediately conveyed directly by the actual words of the sacred writer; second, there is the typical sense when a thing, event or person is used to express something else or to foreshadow some greater truth; then there is the applied sense,wherein concepts, principles, teachings and suggested ideas in a passage are taken by the student or the expositor and applied to life situations.

Always start with the **literal sense**. Other designations for this are grammatical, historical, logical. Words should be taken in their etymological, grammatical, or obvious ordinary meaning.

Next, consider the possible **typical sense**, also sometimes called the spiritual, mystical, allegorical or implied sense.

The **typical sense** is that meaning by which things mentioned signify symbolically, according to the intention of the Holy Spirit, yet other things, but which are founded upon and spring from the literal sense. The person, event or thing which is employed by God to signify something else or foreshadow something else is called a type. The person, event, or thing which is foreshadowed is called the antitype. For example, Adam is a type of Christ, Who is therefore the antitype (Romans 5:14), and the Red Sea is a type of baptism (I Corinthians 10:2), which is the antitype.

How to study primary types

Three things are necessary for a primary type.

First, there must be the real existence of the person, event or thing. In this manner, a primary type differs from metaphors, allegories, or parables, which are mere images without specific historical foundation.

Second, there must be a similarity between the thing which is a type and the thing prefigured by the type. As an illustration, the priesthood of Melchizedek is highly suggestive of the priesthood of Christ. Joseph's life and career contains striking parallels with the Person and ministry of Christ.

Third, it must be God's intention to prefigure, which is normally evidenced by a defining Scripture indicating a typical significance. "Christ our Passover is sacrificed for us," appears in I Corinthians 5:7. By this we know that this important Old Testament event has a typical significance, and therefore looking for comparisons between Christ and the Passover lamb and all of the attendant events is spiritual exercise of great practical value.

Trying to read typical meanings into Scripture where none exist, and supposing that the typical meaning of any passage nullifies the basic literal meaning are dangers to be avoided.

In the applied sense of Scripture, all of the ideas implicit in a passage or suggested in a verse can be taught and related to oneself and to others, including the typical sense. However, it must never be intimated that the applied sense is the sole or true meaning of a passage, but should be clearly expressed as an application of truth for present-day situations.

For instance, the story of Joseph can be used to demonstrate how to turn adversity into prosperity, examining many marvelous techniques and responses the Old Testament hero employed under the blessing and guidance of God to achieve success. This application derives from the historical events, but is not an exposition of the passages. Nor does this approach necessarily involve the typical hallmarks that point to Christ.

In researching the typical meanings, many excellent books will be of value, the most important of which is *Wilson's Dictionary of Types* (Eerdmans), written by Walter Lewis Wilson, MD, DD, a man of spiritual and scientific perceptions. *Cruden's Concordance* contains many fine references to the typical sense of Scripture. A well-stocked Christian bookstore will have several other volumes on biblical Typology, as well.

Trying to read typical meanings into Scripture where none exist, and supposing that the typical meaning of any passage nullifies the basic literal meaning are dangers to be avoided.

Wilson suggests that the student ask himself certain questions as a type is considered:

- How is this object or subject first used in the Scripture? What meaning does it have in the first place where it occurs? [Use your concordance to locate the first mention.]

- To what does this object or subject refer in the last passage where it occurs in the Scripture?

- What are the characteristics of this object or subject which make it a suitable type? Christ is compared to a lion in Revelation 5. In Isaiah 53, Christ is compared to a lamb. As the characteristics of these two animals are studied, the likeness will be more clearly understood. This plan should be followed in each case. [Here, a reading in an encyclopedia about these animals will be most useful as will such research for any object mentioned in the Word.]

- Types should be grouped according to that which they repre-sent. There are types of Christ, Israel, the nations, the Christian, the hypocrites, the worker, the state of the soul, Satan, and many others.

- Types may also be grouped according to their character. There are types taken from the mineral kingdom, the animal kingdom, the vegetable kingdom, the celestial kingdom, the human family, human actions, human attitudes, postures, etc. It will help the student to understand types more fully if these groupings are made while the study is being pursued.

It is also vital to make constant comparisons between an Old Testament type and the New Testament antitype. Write down on a sheet of paper what the Old Testament type is with biblical references, and what the New Testament antitype is with the biblical references.

Also, be on the lookout for these aspects of study:

- Look for opposites, like earthly Jerusalem and heavenly Jerusalem.

- Think of comparisons between Israel's experiences and our experiences.

- Consider the characteristics of the type, such as the sea (Isaiah 57:20), noting its depth, greatness, restlessness, size of waves, commerce, variety (Revelation 17:5). Where does the sea first appear in the Bible? (Study Genesis 1.)

- Think of the lessons that can be drawn from the type and applied to our lives.

How to study secondary types

A secondary type is a person, place, object or thing that is compared by divine inspiration to something else. In this case, there is not necessarily a specific New Testament reference designating the subject as a type. Such secondary types do not necessarily cast a prophetic shadow as does a primary type.

Primary types always prefigure something future. "A Spiritual type and predictive prophecy are in substance the same, differing only in form" (Moorehead).

Figures of speech, likenesses, similes, metaphors and comparisons all come under the category of secondary types. Divinely-inspired symbols are used to convey colorfully-spiritual lesson, divine analysis or practical truth. Therefore, look for the use of the words "as" and "like," which will almost always connote a secondary type, although no direct allusion in the New Testament may appear, corroborating its use.

For instance, "they that wait upon the Lord . . . shall mount up with wings as eagles . . ." is a figurative expression containing a secondary type, likening the believer to an eagle. From the study of the eagle and its similarities with the believer, many practical comparisons and analogies may be made in a strictly devotional and inspirational manner.

Here is a figure of speech in which an historical entity is said to be something else without the use of "as" or "like," the use of which would be naturally implied.

Ephraim is a cake not turned (Hosea 7:8).

Look up Ephraim in this context and discover that here the prophet is using the term to apply to the Northern Kingdom, of which the tribe of Ephraim was the most dominant. Here, the prophet says that the northern nation of Israel (Ephraim) is a cake cooked only on one side. Think of how odd it would seem in a restaurant to be served a pancake with only one side cooked. That side may look very good, but the other side would be unacceptable. The cake would be half-baked. The application is that one side of Ephraim looked good, but the other side, exposed to God, was unacceptable.

Thus, from this historical figure of speech, we can draw the lesson that a person may look very good to other people, but very raw and unacceptable to God who sees things from an upper perspective and not just the downward, or humanward, side.

There are thousands of such figures of speech in the entire Bible.

E. W. Bullinger, in the *Companion Bible,* has a listing of 183 kinds of figures of speech used by ancient Greeks and Hebrews which he suggests are used in the Scripture. It is not necessary to master all of that material, however, to enjoy studying secondary biblical types. Look for the "as" and the "like," or note expressions where a symbol is defined.

Then note when God says that one thing is something else, and an obvious comparison is being made, as in the case of Ephraim above.

How to study parables and allegories

Divinely-inspired illustrations, particularly the parables of Jesus, are not exactly types in the sense we are discussing here, but there is a close kinship. These are illustrations of truths with specific interpretations. Generally, there is a consistency in the use of a symbol, both in the Old Testament types and in the New Testament parables.

For instance, leaven is used as a type or symbol of evil in the Old Testament and the New Testament. It is never a symbol of the growth of God's kingdom or evangelization of the world. Often in the parables, there is a definition of a symbol that is applicable to the study of that type in the Old Testament.

Hebert Lockyer's excellent book *All the Parables of the Bible*, is a most valuable resource book for studying these symbolical stories, as is his work on typology.

We define types as being the Old Testament symbols and metaphors forecasting New Testament realities.

In the parables and comparisons in the New Testament to which no direct reference is made in the Old Testament, there are symbols rather than types. Sometimes, a subject is used throughout the Bible to signify a spiritual reality. For instance, Christ is the Lamb of God all through the Bible, "Christ our passover is sacrificed for us" (1 Cor 5:7).

How to study the Tabernacle

Only the ancient Tabernacle in the wilderness during all of history is divinely designed down to the last detail. Twice in Exodus, we have a description of its structure, use, furniture and importance. If God spends this much time and space on it, the Tabernacle must be very important.

The Book of Hebrews gives us a full explanation of the significance of the famous tent.

Really, the theme, "How can a sinful man approach a holy God?" is developed in Exodus and Leviticus with all of the offerings, ceremonies and officials involved in ancient Israelite worship. Even to the smallest detail, these things relate to the first coming of Christ, the high priesthood of our Savior, the offering of Himself without spot to God, and all that pertains to this very theme.

There are many fine books available in a Christian bookstore on the Tabernacle in the wilderness. Hundreds of truths, lessons, and helpful thoughts can be gleaned from an exhaustive study of this sacred structure

Here are some basics only, for the subject is so vast that hundreds of books have been written on the truths herein revealed:

- Look for Christ in the Tabernacle. He is symbolized by the whole structure. "The Word was made flesh and dwelt [tabernacled] among us" (John 1:14).

- Look for Christ in all the offerings.

- Look for Christ in all the ceremonies.

- Look for Christ in all the garments, ceremonies and responsibilities of the high priest.

Compare the events of the last week of our Lord, the Book of Hebrews, and all references by Paul and John to the typical meanings of Old Testament events.

Remember that *"what things soever were written aforetime, were written for our learning, that we through patience and comfort of the Scriptures might have hope"* (Romans 15:4).

J. Sidlow Baxter (*Studies in Problem Texts*) commented on the absence of the teaching of types in the church today, calling it, "The generality of modern pulpits!" It is a regrettable omission for two reasons outstandingly: (1) because the type content of the Old Testament furnishes a grand proof of its inspiration, being the most wonderful of all forms of prophecy, and (2) because it invests the New Testament with an endless new wealth of meaning for ourselves today. There seems to be a strange ignorance even of the presence of such type-teaching in the Old Testament.

The Greek word *tupoi* is translated in the KJV as *ensamples* as in the following verse:

Now, all these things happened unto them for ensamples: and they are written for our admonition, upon whom the ends of the world are come (I Corinthians 10:11).

Study the types of the Bible! There is no more rewarding nor illuminating study in all the Word of God.

Which things we also speak, not in the words which man's wisdom teacheth, but which the Holy Ghost teacheth; comparing spiritual things with spiritual (I Corinthians 2:13).

10

HOW TO STUDY BIBLE NUMBERS

Closely associated with biblical typology, and thought by some expositors to be included in it, is the study of numbers in Scripture. No one can be a serious student of Holy Writ and fail to see the symbolical significance of certain prime or important numbers such as 7, 12 and 40, which are used so frequently in the Word, but a careful consideration of how other numbers are used will also yield fascinating spiritual lessons.

Again, it is wise to approach this subject with caution, lest with excessive eagerness concepts could be read into Scripture which are really not there.

Not only are numbers significant but so are geometrical forms, thus showing how the Master Mathematician and Geometrician has designed His revelation to mankind with precision, beauty and symmetry.

In all of nature, the great Creator has designed His creatures with balance, measurable numerical laws, and in fantastic geometrical forms.

Seven is significant.

Seven notes in music provide an almost infinite variety for harmony and song with the octave, the eighth note, being a repeat of the first in a higher key, a new beginning.

When white light is transformed into its rainbow colors, seven basic tones are visible, so radiantly symmetrical that no one can fail to see their beauty.

It is important that we consider the existence and meaning of these following numbers:

ONE . . .unity
One is the number standing for unity, an important idea in the Bible.

Hear, O Israel, the LORD our God is one LORD (Deut. 6:4).

Take your concordance and look up every instance where ONE is mentioned. In Ephesians 4:1-6, the sevenfold UNITY of the church is stressed. "There is ONE body, and ONE Spirit, even as ye are called in ONE hope of your calling; ONE Lord, ONE faith, ONE baptism, ONE God and Father of all."

Where outside of Christ there are Jews and Gentiles, in Christ, *"He is our peace, who hath made both ONE, and hath broken down the middle wall of partition between us"* (Ephesians 2:14).

Looking forward to the ultimate assembly of all believers in heaven, Christ prayed, *"Neither pray I for these alone, but for them which shall believe on me through their word: that they all may be ONE" (John 17:20,21).*

In the number ONE, the idea of UNITY also implies *supremacy, exclusivity* and *independency*.

These things are true in the highest sense only of God, but in lesser realms, the principle is the same.

TWO . . . difference or division

This number is plainly the opposite of ONE, which speaks of UNITY. If ONE excludes difference, TWO affirms it. If ONE says there is not another, TWO says there is another. Therefore TWO may imply enmity and conflict in its *primary application.*

Adam and Eve had TWO sons initially, Cain and Abel, who contrast by their personalities and actions: the righteous and the wicked. The Bible speaks of the WAY OF CAIN versus RIGHTEOUS ABEL.

Genesis 10:25 says, "And unto Eber were born *two* sons: the name of one was Peleg; for in his day was the earth DIVIDED: and his brother's name was Joktan." Here, early on in the Scripture, the number two is associated with DIVISION.

Consider other opposite pairs, like Ishmael and Isaac, Jacob and Esau, the Northern Kingdom and the Southern Kingdom, all teaching the contrast between RIGHTEOUS and WICKED. Throughout the Word, the division continues, frequently suggesting that there is a *broad road* that leads to *destruction* and a *narrow road* that leads to *life.*

But there is a secondary application for the number TWO. It can speak of combination, witness or testimony.

That in the mouth of two or three witnesses, every word should be established (Matthew 18:16).

Jesus sent out the Twelve and the Seventy on a two-by-two basis for witnessing and preaching. In marriage, the two become one flesh. Evangelistic teams like Paul and Barnabas, and later, Paul and Silas were more effective than a single voice for God. Even Jesus said the Father did bear witness to Him and that "I and my Father are One."

THREE . . . the Trinity and resurrection

Standing for the TRINITY and RESURRECTION, the number THREE carries the idea of fullness, actuality; the ideas of solidity, reality and substance are associated with the number.

THREE dimensions are necessary for reality: length, height, and width. Time exists in three tenses: past, present and future. Matter is found in three forms: solids, liquids and gasses. Reflecting the divine TRINITY, the whole universe hangs on these basic threes.

Christ, who was the fullness of the Godhead bodily, was raised from the dead the THIRD DAY. Jonah was THREE days and nights in the belly of the fish, typifying Christ's THREE days and nights in the tomb. Our Lord raised THREE persons from the grave. There are THREE recorded cases of resurrection in the Old Testament. The first was the son of the widow of Zarephath (I Kings 17), raised by the prophet Elijah, who stretched himself THREE times upon the child.

The second case was performed by Elisha, who raised the dead son of the Shulamite woman (2 Kings 4). The last was the case of the dead man revived by touching the bones of Elisha (2 Kings 13:21).

Look up other cases where a THREE is emphasized (Genesis 18:22; Joshua 3; 2 Corinthians 12). Use your concordance and *Wilson's Dictionary of Types* for further research on this number.

FOUR . . . the world

In Revelation 7:1, we read of the "four winds of the earth," indicating the FOUR directions. In Daniel 2 and 7, we read of FOUR great world civilizations, compared to FOUR METALS and to FOUR BEASTS, all dealing with the Gentile world dominion during "the times of the Gentiles."

During the Dispensation of Grace, the gospel is preached in this field, which is the world (Matthew 13), and there are FOUR kinds of soil, FOUR types of response that may be expected.

By way of illustration, and most curiously, man is associated in this world with FOURS.

When we are born, we are laid in a four-cornered bed and soon learn to crawl on all fours. We live in four-cornered rooms, eat at four-cornered tables, and sit on four-cornered chairs. We look out four-cornered windows, walk through four-cornered doors and retire on four-cornered beds.

We ride in four-wheeled cars, move in four directions, work at four-cornered desks, read from four-cornered papers, and correspond in four-cornered envelopes and look at four-cornered screens.

As we reach the point of death, we may lie on a four-cornered embalming table, then we are placed in a four-cornered coffin, transported in a four-wheeled hearse to a four-cornered grave, where a four-cornered spade then covers us up.

FIVE . . . divine grace versus human experience

In the Pentateuch, the first five books of the Bible, the law is set forth which reveals man's sins and shows his basic human weakness. On each hand, humans have FIVE fingers, showing that this limits their potential. Only so much can be done with human hands. There are FIVE books of PSALMS, as indicated in the Scofield Bible, for instance, within which both human limitations and God's mercy (grace) are revealed.

There were FIVE foolish virgins and FIVE wise virgins in Matthew 25, again demonstrating both human weakness and divine grace. In Leviticus 1-5, we read of FIVE basic offerings which were observed at the Tabernacle, revealing human weakness and divine grace. When David prepared for his confrontation with Goliath, he picked up FIVE smooth stones, suggesting that his weakness would be offset by God's grace. He also may have been thinking about Goliath's four brothers.

SIX . . . man

Now we come to the number SIX which deals with man, especially in his fallen state and as influenced by Satan.

SIX days make up man's week of labor—a labor that has come through sin.

The number of the beast, 666 (Revelation 13), whatever else it may signify, does speak of the full development of sinful man under the control of Satan in the very highest opposition to God.

Man was created on the sixth day (Genesis 1).

SEVEN . . . completeness or perfection

SEVEN, denoting completeness or perfection, is the most-emphasized number in the Bible. In Genesis, the SEVEN days of creation introduce us to the completed earth. God resting on the SEVENTH day indicates His special use of this number, establishing the principle that one day in SEVEN belongs to God.

There are sets of SEVENS to be found all through the Bible. The seventy SEVENS (weeks) of Daniel, the SEVEN sayings from the Cross, the SEVEN parables of the kingdom of heaven (Matthew 13), the SEVEN petitions in the Lord's Prayer are a few of the examples to be found in the Word.

In the book of Revelation, the number SEVEN appears 54 times, together with several sets of SEV-ENS that must be researched to find, like the SEVEN voices in chapter 14. In this last climactic book of the Bible, we find such references as SEVEN churches, SEVEN stars, SEVEN angels of the churches, SEVEN seals, SEVEN trumpets, SEVEN lamps of fire, SEVEN thunders, SEVEN thousands, SEVEN heads (on the dragon and on the beast), SEVEN vials, SEVEN angels of the judgment, and there are SEVEN new things in chapters 21 and 22. Study the SEVEN last sayings of Christ in the end of the book for an additional blessing.

Seven notes in music provide an almost infinite variety for harmony and song with the octave, the eighth note, being a repeat of the first in a higher key, a new beginning. When white light is transformed into its rainbow colors, seven basic tones are visible, so radiantly symmetrical that no one can fail to see their beauty.

EIGHT . . . new things

The first day of the week is the EIGHTH day after the start of a preceding week, marking a new beginning. Jesus arose therefore on the

EIGHTH DAY, the firstfruits, the first-begotten from the dead. He founded a whole new spiritual race, the redeemed of the ages.

Noah was the EIGHTH person, and he began a new era in human history. EIGHT people were on the ark, the founders of a new civilization. Circumcision, a sign and seal of God's covenant, was performed on males on the EIGHTH day.

David was the EIGHTH son of Jesse and he founded a new dynasty.

In our Lord's conversation with Nicodemus on the new birth, the word *born* occurs EIGHT times.

NINE . . . The Holy Spirit

Coming after EIGHT, which suggests the new birth, the number NINE seems to be associated with the Holy Spirit.

There are NINE virtues listed as the fruit of the Spirit in Galatians 5:22,23: love, joy, peace, longsuffering, gentleness, goodness, faith, meekness, temperance (self-control).

There are NINE gifts of the Spirit in I Corinthians 12.

There are NINE beatitudes spoken by our Lord in Matthew 5 which, when experienced in the believer's life, are a result of the Holy Spirit working in our lives.

TEN . . . the Law

There were TEN commandments setting forth God's basic standard for righteousness in the Law.

When the Passover lamb was selected (Exodus 12:6) on the TENTH day, it was then kept until the fourteenth day for sacrifice. "Christ, our Passover, was sacrificed for us," thus paying the penalty the Law demands for our sins.

TWELVE . . .divine government

TWELVE is the number for government by divine appointment. Jesus said to His apostles, "Verily I say unto you, that ye which have followed me, in the regeneration when the Son of man shall sit on the throne of his glory, ye shall also sit on TWELVE thrones, judging the TWELVE tribes of Israel" (Matthew 19:28).

Note that TWELVE can be the total of FIVE (God's grace) and

SEVEN (God's perfection) which together result in God's divine government.

Thus, the higher numbers are the sum and product of the lower numbers and are variations that combine truths.

FORTY . . . testing

Our Savior was tempted forty days and forty nights by the devil (Matthew 4). Moses spent FORTY years at the backside of the desert, resisting temptation and being spiritually prepared to be the emancipator of Israel. Moses was 40 days in the mountain receiving the Law, but the delivered Israelites failed the test and fell into idolatry while he was gone (Exodus 32).

SEVENTY . . . Israel's punishment and restoration

God deals with Israel in SEVENTY-year periods and in multiples of SEVEN, such as SEVENTY times SEVEN, or 490 years.

Israel's SEVENTY years of Babylonian captivity lasted from 606 to 536 B.C., during which the land kept its Sabbaths to make up for the 490 previous years when the sabbatical years were not observed. Some think that 490 years elapsed between the Exodus and Saul's reign, and that there were 490 years stretching from Abraham to the Exodus.

Even before the TWELVE tribes of Israel divided by divine appointment the promised land, there had been TWELVE princes of Ishmaelic descent (Genesis 17:20).

Solomon had TWELVE officers over all Israel (I Kings 4:7).

The capital city of the universe, New Jerusalem, center of God's cosmic government, will have TWELVE foundations and TWELVE gates of pearl with the name of the TWELVE tribes and the TWELVE apostles most prominent.

Now notice that EIGHT is the sum of SEVEN (which signifies divine completion and perfection) and ONE (which speaks of UNITY), which together suggest a divinely-appointed new beginning or new birth.

Remember that NINE is the sum of FOUR (meaning the world) and FIVE, typifying God's grace triumphant over human weakness. Since the Holy Spirit is associated with NINE, His indwelling power enables us to experience the power of His grace in the midst of a wicked world, exhibiting the fruit of the Spirit.

TEN, speaking of the Law, is the sum of FOUR (the world) and SIX (sinful man), thus suggesting that the Law condemns sinful man in this world.

The famous prophecy of the SEVENTY WEEKS of Daniel 9 pinpoints the first coming of Christ. During that period, which began about 450 B.C. in the days of Ezra and Nehemiah and continued to the coming of Christ, a total of 69 WEEKS (SEVENS) of years transpired, 483 years all total, according to the prophecy, at the end of which the Messiah would come. That brings us to about A.D. 33.

The final SEVEN, or WEEK OF YEARS, is the tribulation time further expanded and explained in the book of Revelation. Compare Daniel 9:27 with Revelation 6:18.

Summing up

These numbers are the principal ones in the Word of God. Use your concordance and look up all these numbers for yourself. Some commentators have speculated that there are special meanings in many other numbers mentioned throughout the 1,189 chapters of the Bible, but this writer believes that going much beyond what is plainly set forth can lead to fanciful imagination.

Now, no one believes that the chapter divisions made by Archbishop Stephen Lancton in England during the 12th century are inspired in the same sense that the original Greek and Hebrew autographs were God-breathed, but in studying the Bible for these many decades, this writer has found a curious fact. Test it yourself as you research the Word. Certain chapters seem to confirm and corroborate these numerical studies.

Every chapter ONE in the Bible contains something about God, often pointing up His unity and sovereignty.

Every chapter TWO contains a contrast between the righteous and the wicked, or what is right and what is wrong, or something relating to witness or testimony.

Every chapter THREE in the New Testament either mentions or suggests the Trinity.

Every chapter FOUR contains something about the world or those that are in it, true in the Old Testament and the New.

Every chapter FIVE presents a contrast between God's grace and human weakness. For instance, Genesis 5 tells of ancients who died after long lives, indicating their ultimate weakness as sinful humans. But there is the account of Enoch who did not die, for he walked with God and was translated by faith (Hebrews 11), a picture of grace.

Every chapter SIX mentions some interesting fact about man, usually demonstrating that he is a sinner.

Every chapter SEVEN shows something wonderful about God or His attributes.

Every chapter EIGHT contains some new thing not previously revealed clearly in the Word.

Perhaps it is only a coincidence. Why not go through the Bible and see if these things are

Use your concordance and look up all these numbers for yourself. Some commentators have speculated that there are special meanings in many other numbers mentioned throughout the 1,189 chapters of the Bible, but this writer believes that going much beyond what is plainly set forth can lead to fanciful imagination.

true. Find in each chapter what we suggest, up through the eighth chapters.

Then you can judge for yourself.

NUMBERS IN REVELATION

No reader of the Apocalypse has failed to notice the frequent recurrence of numbers which appear to carry with them a certain symbolical meaning.

The following are the numbers that are mentioned in the book: 2, 3, 3 1/2, 4, 5, 6, 7, 10, 12, 24, 42, 144, 666 (or according to another reader, 616), 1000, 1260, 1600, 7000, 12,000; 144,000; 100,000,000; 200,000,000. The predominant number is *seven*, which occurs 54 times. The book is addressed to seven Churches represented by seven lampstands, while their 'angels' are seven stars. There are seven Spirits of God, symbolized by seven lamps. The Book in the Hand of God is sealed with seven seals; the Lamb before the Throne has seven eyes and seven horns. Seven angels blow seven trumpet blasts; seven other angels pour out the contents of seven bowls full of seven last plagues. Seven thunders utter voices which the Seer is bidden not to write. Seven thousand are killed in the great earthquake which follows the ascension of the Two Witnesses. The Dragon has seven heads, and upon them seven diadems; the Wild Beast from the Sea has seven heads on which are "names of blasphemy"; the Scarlet Beast on which Babylon sits has likewise seven heads, variously interpreted by the writer as seven mountains, or seven kings. Next in frequency to the *heptad* is the *dodecad*. Israel consists of *twelve* tribes; as in the Woman in 12:1. The New Jerusalem has twelve portals, and the wall that girdles it rests on twelve foundation stones on which are engraved the names of the twelve Apostles; the Tree of Life in the new Paradise bears twelve manners of fruits, after the number of months. Multiples of twelve, also, are common. Each of the tribes of Israel contains 12,000, making a total of 144,000; and 144,000 is also the number which in the second part of the book are seen surrounding the Lamb on Mount Zion. The Elders around the Throne are 24, and they are seated on as many subordinate thrones. Each side of the Holy City is 12,000 furlongs in length. The wall which surrounds it is 144 cubits in height.

–H. B. Swete

11

HOW TO STUDY BIBLE PROPHECY

Unique to biblical Christianity is the positive feature of fulfilled prophecy. No other religious system contains more than a smattering of prophetic generalizations, whereas our theology includes literally hundreds of prophecies, often forecasts of events hundreds and thousands of years in the future. About half of biblical prophecy is already fulfilled, much of it dealing with the first coming of Christ.

Some three hundred thirty-three specific facts about the birth, life, character and work of Christ are spelled out in detail throughout the Old Testament; including the Second Coming.

Mathematically, the probability of all these prophecies coming into focus on one person at one point in time is so astronomical that any thinking person must acknowledge that there is a supernatural element in Bible prophecy.

A true prophecy must be beyond the realm of *human calculation*. No one could just carefully analyze the trends and calculate a conclusion.

A true prophecy must be beyond the realm of *human collusion*. If several persons are cooperating to fulfill a prophecy by pre-planned design, then no supernatural element would exist.

A true prophecy must be beyond the realm of *human comprehension*. If a man could by merely natural means comprehend the scope of prophecy, accurately foretelling the future with human insights, then again there is no divine inspiration.

A true prophecy must be beyond the realm of *human cooperation*. Often Bible prophecy involves people who would be antipathetic to God's will, and therefore not likely to cooperate with one of His prophets to bring an event or circumstance to pass.

How to study fulfilled prophecy

Christ's first coming is foretold in the Old Testament. A topical Bible (*Zondervan's* or *Nave's*) contains hundreds of verses on Christ in the Old Testament. *All the Prophecy*, by Herbert Lockyer, is an excellent source book for prophetic studies.

You can go through the entire New Testament with the aid of a concordance and other reference books, searching for *quotations and allusions to the Old Testament*. Matthew, written especially to present the Messiah to the Jews, is full of such quotations. They differ slightly in wording or grammatical construction because they were quoted from the Greek translation of the Old Testament known as the Septuagint, rather than from the original Hebrew, since Matthew was published in Greek. In some New Testaments, 305 quotations from the Old Testament are italicized or highlighted. Revelation contains 278 allusions to the Old Testament with only one quotation in full (*Babylon the great is fallen, is fallen*).

Read through the Old Testament prophets.
Write down all predictions of Christ in Isaiah, for instance, noting especially those already and obviously fulfilled. Follow suit with all the other prophets. A good reference Bible will be most useful in this investigation.

Look for *political prophecies* concerning ancient nations, and note their fulfillment both from Scripture and secular history. Nahum, for instance, announces the doom of Ninevah. Some decades after he wrote, the city was conquered and destroyed, exactly as predicted.

Study the nation of Israel
Beginning in Genesis, give special attention to the predictions of Jacob in Genesis 49. Remember that the prophets primarily spoke to and about Israel in ancient times, touching on other world powers when they had some relationship to His earthly chosen people.

Write down one very important principle.
When the Old Testament speaks in prophetic terms describing the future, *it is always a literal prediction about a literal event (or events).* When Jeremiah prophesied the 70 years of captivity, he was not presenting some

mystic truth with a cryptic meaning. Making ordinary allowances for obvious figurative language, interpret the Word of God precisely as written. Fulfilled prophecy always came to pass literally and factually.

How to study unfulfilled prophecy

The previously-mentioned principle still applies to future prophesied events.

Remember again the basic importance for understanding the Bible. "If the plain sense of Scripture makes common sense, seek no other sense. Therefore, take every word at its primary, ordinary, literal meaning unless the immediate context of the Scripture, studied in the light of axiomatic, fundamental truths, clearly indicates a figurative interpretation."

Prophecies of the future will be fulfilled just as literally as those that happened in the Old Testament times and in the first coming of Jesus Christ.

That is logical, sensible and correct.

It is also important to recognize the Law of Double Reference, which is "the principle of associating similar ideas which are usually separated from one another by long periods of time, but which may be blended into a single picture initially, and in which a historical past even may illustrate a future prophetic event."

From 1 Peter 1:10-11, we learn that even the prophets wondered about the sufferings of Christ and the glory that should follow. In Isaiah, prophecies of Christ's first coming and predictions of His future glory are sometimes blended in the same context. From our vantage point in time, we can observe that there is an interval, the church age, between the "sufferings of Christ" at His first coming and "the glory of Christ" at His return.

Studying the Old Testament prophecies

Look up the expressions, "the day of the Lord," and "that day." (Use your concordance or topical Bible.) Almost always these refer to the end times, the conclusion of history as we have known it, sometimes referring to what Jesus called the "great tribulation," sometimes describing the glory of Israel's future under the Messiah-King.

Give special attention to the apocalyptic approach of Daniel, portions

of Ezekiel, and much of Zechariah, all of which have much to say about
the end of the age.

Considering the time prophecies of Daniel.

The incredible prediction of Daniel nine, concerning
the famous SEVENTY WEEKS or SEVENTY SEVENS—490 years—is
worthy of intense examination. That 69 weeks of years or 483 years was to elapse from the "going forth of the commandment to restore and build Jerusalem" unto "the Messiah" is a powerful proof of divine inspiration. About 457 B.C., Ezra came to usher in a revival in the restored, post-captivity, subordinate nation of Israel. Nehemiah came about 445 B.C. as the governor and to rebuild the walls of Jerusalem under the authority of the Persian king.

Unique to biblical Christianity is the positive feature of fulfilled prophecy. No other religious system contains more than a smattering of prophetic generalizations, whereas our theology includes literally hundreds of prophecies, often forecasts of events hundreds and thousands of years in the future.

If you start with this time period at about 450 B.C. and move forward
in time 483 years, you came to 33 B.C. about the time Jesus was crucified.
Some authorities, like Gleason L. Archer, begin the 483-year period at
about 457, and move in calendar years of 365 days forward to about A.D.
27 when Jesus was baptized. Sir Robert Anderson, using the ancient
Jewish year of 360 days, has calculated that 483 years of 360 days each,
beginning in 445 B.C. brings us to the exact time of Jesus' crucifixion,
which he places about A.D. 30.

While some scholars differ on the details, and given the fact that the
ancient calendars may have been off a few years, there is still the profound
fact that Jesus Christ, the Messiah, did come, fulfilling many other Old
Testament Scriptures, 69 weeks (of years) or 483 years after the days of
Ezra and Nehemiah.

Some believe that 457 B.C. is the starting point and that A.D. 27
when Jesus was baptized and began his public ministry was the terminus
of the 483 ordinary calendar years of 365 days each.

The "seventieth seven," or "seventieth week of Daniel," is the final seven years of prophesied history as we know it.

In his commentary on Daniel, most of which has been lost, Hypolytus, writing in about A.D. 220, teaches this very truth, explaining that the book of Revelation is an expansion on Daniel 9:27. Hypolytus was a disciple of Irenaeus, who was a disciple of Polycarp, who was a disciple of John the Revelator. The circumstantial probability of a continuous succession of teaching is a strong argument for our present position. He pointed out the significance of the "42 months," the "1,260 days) was the "Time of Elijah," whom he saw as one of the two witnesses of Revelation 11. The later three-and-a-half years he described as the "time of the Antichrist."

This early apostolic and post-apostolic teaching was lost and rejected after the Christianization of the Roman Empire. Many of the later post-Nicene fathers (spiritual leaders and writers in the fourth and fifth centuries) supposed that the conversion of the Roman Empire and western civilization to Christianity was the prophesied millennium.

While not totally forgotten, this truth of the end times was revived in the 18th and 19th century, and has become a vital part of our understanding of prophecy.

Compare the prophetic preaching of Jesus.
Particularly in Matthew 24 and 25, Mark 13, and Luke 17 and 21, with the theme and thrust of the book of Revelation. Look up the references in writings of Paul, especially in I and 2 Thessalonians, and in the statements of Peter, James, John and Jude about the second coming. Look for a total pattern. All of the prophecies work together to form a logical network of prophetic truth.

Make a special project of studying the book of Revelation.
There are many fine commentaries by such notables as W. A. Criswell past-pastor of the First Baptist Church of Dallas; Walter Scott, a great scholar of yesteryear, and the incomparable Joseph Seiss, whose masterful and eloquent work entitled *The Apocalypse*, was published over a hundred years ago, but still is relevant, timely and informative.

Recent books by Tim LaHaye, Jim Combs and Robert Thomas on Revelation are available. Thomas' 2-volume work is the most detailed and scholarly commentary yet written.

Closing observations

Study prophecy for what it is, prewritten history, believing the unfulfilled and future prophecies as equally inspired, basically literal, and certain as those already fulfilled.

Study prophecy without searching for new revelations undiscovered by great eschatological scholars and writers. Attempts to read into the Word of God copious references to America under some mystical name will lead to highly speculative conclusions. Far-out mathematical calculations aimed at setting a date for the return of Christ are an extreme to be avoided. History is strewn with the theological corpses of date-setting theories.

Study prophecy, particularly references to the "rapture" and the "glorious appearing," noting that the concept of a sudden, secret, surprising coming *for the saints* (I Thessalonians 4:17,18) is to be distinguished from the open, climactic coming of Christ *with the saints* (2 Thessalonians 1:7-10). Incidentally, the word "rapture," which does not appear in the King James Version, is from a Latin word for "caught up" (*rapeo*), that appeared in the Latin Vulgate, which was the Bible of western Europe for a thousand years.

Study prophecy, not just as a curiosity-seeker or a dabbler in the mysteries of God, but with the motivation to serve God more vigorously until He comes.

The *Tim LaHaye Prophecy Study Bible*, originally published by AMG is now available through David Wood Ministries, at www.DWministries.org.

This work, completed in 2000, was edited by Tim LaHaye, Ed Hindson, Thomas Ice, and James Combs. It also contains 84 special articles on prophetic subjects by outstanding scholars, authors, and teachers.

Another useful tool for prophetic studies is *The Prophecy Study Bible* edited by Grant R. Jeffrey.

12

How to Study Bible Persons

The Bible is about people in all kinds of situations, people with problems, people with needs, people who are examples, people who succeeded, people who failed, people who followed God and people who did not.

Studying Bible personalities is both fascinating and profitable.

Throughout the Scriptures, one supreme Person stands out as the Lord of life and the ideal Example. Christ, the Savior, is the central personality of the Bible. Our study of persons will culminate by considering Him.

How to study Old Testament personalities
Why not start with Adam, the first person God created for this earth?

Look up his name in a Strong's Concordance.
Other studies can follow the same general guidelines. His name appears some 24 times in the Old Testament; 8 times in the New Testament. Of course, the pronoun "he," referring to Adam, appears in Genesis several times.

Find the meaning of the name in your Bible dictionary.
Read there what the writer says about the personality. Make notes (never forget to have paper and pencil right there to jot down thoughts and ideas) from this biographical account.

Compare, if possible, any information about him you can glean from other sources you have available.
Read about Adam in your one-volume commentary, looking up the various places where he is mentioned.

Think on his life.

Start with the positive side. Ask these questions about Adam (or any other person you are studying):

Why was this person mentioned?

Why was he different from any other person in the Bible?

What were his beginnings or origins or ancestry?

What were the good qualities about him? List them.

What were the negative characteristics in his life—mistakes, problems, sins?

Did he do anything to counteract these negatives?

What was his relationship to God?

What heritage did he leave for successive generations?

What descriptive words best suggest his total character?

What relationship did he have to Christ, if any?

You may think of other thought–provoking questions about your character. Make up a list of questions you can ask about each personality you study. Here are a few more possibilities:

What journeys did the character make?

What relationships with others did he build? Positive or negative?

What problems did he solve or fail to solve?

What examples did he leave that are good for me to follow?

What mistakes did he make that I ought to avoid?

Was he a person typical of others today?

Does he typify Christ in any way (like Moses, Aaron, David, etc.)?

Look for unusual things about persons. All the prominent people in the Bible have certain strong and distinctive characteristics. Search for the different, the strange, even the bizarre. This will prove most interesting.

If available, use any other reference books with biographical studies.

The late Herbert Lockyer, who went to be with Christ at the age of 95, left a vast legacy in his *"All"* series. His volumes, *All the Men of the Bible, All the Women of the Bible, All the Kings and Queens of the Bible,* and other studies in personalities are well worth the monetary investment and reading time.

How to study New Testament personalities

Consideration of people in the New Testament differs from the Old

Testament biographies because of the new and unique relationship to Christ that some persons in this dispensation enjoy.

Follow the same general procedures listed above for other biographical studies.

Look up the name in Strong's concordance and your Nave's (Zondervan's) Topical Bible.
Read excerpts from various books in the Bible that mention his name.

Find the meaning of the name in your Bible dictionary.
Often the significance of the name is a clue to the character and conduct of the person. This is true in the Old Testament as well.

For instance, Jacob means "a supplanter," one who takes the place of another, sometimes by force or cunning. Does this apply to Jacob? Israel, God's new name for him, denotes "prince with God." What does this teach?

And in the New Testament, find the meaning of Saul. Compare "Paul," which was the great apostle's name during his spiritual career. Is there any significance in this?

Find and read biographical sketches of any person you are studying.
Use any and/or all reference books available.

Think on the life of the person.
Use thought-provoking, stimulating questions such as those above, and write down your responses and the results of your prayerful research.

Do not neglect obscure names and persons.
In the New Testament, for instance, there is a *Secundus*, a *Tertius*, and a *Quartus*, which mean "second," "third," and "fourth." Find out why these unusual names were used and what these persons did for Christ, if anything.

Compare the lives and characters of the persons before they met Christ and after they met Christ.
List changes and differences.

Make up an outline study of the person's life.
You may have available F.E. Marsh's volumes, still in print, *500 Bible*

Outlines and *1,000 Bible Outlines.*

There you will find many interesting outlines on Bible characters most useful for personal meditation and sharing with others.

Here are two examples:

ABEL, THE MAN OF FAITH

The Man of Faith acts according to God's Word
(Hebrews 11:4).

The Man of Faith is regarded by God (Genesis 4:4).

The Man of Faith is envied by others (Genesis 4:4).

The Man of Faith condemns the unrighteous (I John 3:12).

The Man of Faith is noted by God (Matthew 23:55; Luke 11:51;
Hebrews 11:4; 12:24, etc).

CAIN, THE MAN OF UNBELIEF

The Man of Unbelief acts in his own way (Jude 11;
Proverbs 14:12).

The Man of Unbelief is rejected (Genesis 4:5).

The Man of Unbelief is self-willed (Genesis 4:7).

The Man of Unbelief is unhappy (Genesis 4:5,6).

The Man of Unbelief is hateful (Genesis 4:8).

The Man of Unbelief is punished (Genesis 4:11-13).

What other thoughts are suggested in these two personalities? What
is the "way of Cain" (Jude 11)? Why was Abel "righteous?"

Do these two men exemplify two spiritual roads? How does the New
Testament depict these contrasting paths? What did each trust for accept-
ance with God? How does the New Testament relate to these things?

With thousands of names in the Bible and hundreds of significant
persons to be studied, the Bible researcher will gain a wealth of spiritual instruction by learning all that is possible about these fascinating people
of the Bible.

How to study the life of Christ

Since the Bible is about Jesus, much time should be spent considering
Him.

What to use in studying the life of Christ.
You may want to use a red-letter edition which gives the words of Christ in color. You may want to use one Bible for this study, marking much in it and running many cross-references. Read all four Gospels.

Get a Harmony of the Gospels.
This will enable you to read through the life of Christ in chronological order. You will find it at your local Christian bookstore.

Get a map of the Holy Land in the time of Christ.
Trace the journeys of Christ. Use your Bible geography or atlas, one of the basic tools you should have in your minimal library.

Look at photographs of Bible places.
The American Bible Society published a magazine-sized New Testament (KJV) with pictures of places on nearly all the pages. This will help you get the feel of the land and the locations where events took place. You may find some other illustrated New Testament or study of Christ's life that will likewise provide insights about the land.

For more advanced students, get W. Graham Scroggie's book, Guide to the Gospels.
This book contains invaluable information not to be found in any other work in print.

Study each Gospel separately.
They are portraits of Christ, each geared for a different audience.

As you study Matthew's Gospel, look up all references to the Old Testament. List them. How many are there? How many books are quoted? What are some of the problem references? To whom did Matthew write, initially and primarily? What are the key words and expressions? List them. How does Matthew present Christ?

When reading Mark's Gospel, note the recurrence of the words "immediately," "forthwith," and "straightway." Why are these words used? By the way, in the Greek they are all the same basic word. To whom was Mark appealing with his presentation? How does he present the Savior?

Perusing Luke's Gospel, the longest of the four, leads the reader to see Christ as the perfect man. How does Luke introduce his writing?

The first three are sometimes called the "synoptic" Gospels, because they contain a synopsis of Christ's life.

The Gospel of John is different. Look for key words. Find the eight miracles. Consider the special teachings in this book about the Holy Spirit. To whom was John writing?

Read an introduction to each of these Gospels in your Bible dictionary.

Make up chapter headings for each of the 89 chapters and form a simple outline of each book. Always write down your thoughts and findings.

Study your Harmony of the Gospels.
Read it through over a period of a few days or weeks. Compare the alternate presentations which each writer makes of the same events. How does that prove inspiration? Would people writing from different viewpoints for different purposes explain events with different emphases?

Look carefully at how Jesus changed his approach and messages as rejection of Messiah by the Jews became more evident. Were there special times when Christ began new emphases? How does the Sermon on the Mount (Matthew 5:7) differ from the Upper Room Discourse (John 14-16)? Write down the differences and think on the audiences and the times.

Consider the periods of His ministry.
After looking at the ancestry, birth and early life of Christ, notice these specific preaching tours:

- The Early Perean Ministry
- The Early Galilean Ministry
- The Early Judean Ministry
- The Samaritan Ministry
- The Great Galilean Ministry
- The Later Judean Ministry
- The Later Perean Ministry
- The Final Jerusalem Ministry

Then study carefully all the events of the Last Week.

Another way to view the life and ministry of Christ is to notice:

- The Birth of Christ
- The Childhood of Christ
- The Baptism of Christ
- The Year of Obscurity
- The Year of Opportunity
- The Year of Opposition
- The Last Week
- The Crucifixion
- The Resurrection
- The Appearances
- The Ascension
- Present Ministry of Intercession

Find and read a book on the life of Christ
Consult a good Christian bookstore to find a reverent and spiritual study, since compositions by liberal writers may find their way to even Christian bookstore shelves. Buy wisely. An old work with vast scholarship and research behind it and which is still in print is entitled *Life and Times of Jesus the Messiah*, by Alfred Edersheim. It is well worth plowing through, 100-word sentences and extensive vocabulary notwithstanding. But start with something simpler. You might want to ask your pastor what book he would recommend.

Follow up your study.
Remember that Paul and the other apostles interpreted the meaning of the life and ministry of Christ. Do not forget to use your topical Bible, looking up JESUS CHRIST, reading all of the Scriptures listed there about our Savior for additional information and impact.

Finally, John the Revelator gives us the final destiny and glory of Christ in the last book in the Bible. Read and mediate on Revelation 1, which depicts the ascended, glorified Prophet, Priest and Prince, the King of Kings and Lord of Lords. Find the seven last sayings of Christ in the close of the book. Resolve to love, follow, serve, obey, worship and admire Him forever.

Christ as the Boy of Nazareth

How many stars shine in the sky of Christ's early days as the Boy of the humble home of Nazareth? Read Luke 2.

1. The Growing Child. The Child grew, He was supernatural in His being as "The Son," but He was perfectly natural in His childhood.
2. The Strong Spirit. "Waxed strong in spirit." The spirit nature in man is evidenced in his individuality and in his intelligence—see 1 Corinthians 2: 11.
3. The Wise Mind. "Filled with wisdom." To be wise is good, but to be filled with wisdom is better. Wisdom is the right application of knowledge.
4. The Graced Boy. "The grace of God was upon Him."
5. The True Israelite. He went with His parents to Jerusalem to keep the Passover—41, 42.
6. The Tarrying Lad—43. The reason why He tarried is given by Himself. He felt He Must be about About His Father's business—49. The consciousness He had come into the world to do a definite work pressing upon Him.
7. The Missed Son—43-45. The parents of jesus lost Him one day, and it took three days to find Him. They supposed He was with them, but suppositions do not make realities. It takes a longer time to recover our blessings than it does to lose them.
8. The Central Figure—47. He was found "in the midst" of the doctors, "hearing them, asking them questions."
9. The Higher Relationship—49. How startled Mary must have been when she heard the words: "Wist ye not I must be about My Father's business?" especially following her statement: "Thy father and I have sought Thee sorrowing."

13

HOW TO STUDY A BIBLE DOCTRINE

The word, "Doctrine" is derived from the Latin word *doctrina* which, in turn, is based on the word *docco*, meaning "to teach." A doctrine is a major teaching of the Scriptures or the totality of what is taught in the Scriptures. "Doctor" is linked to the same word and signifies "teacher."

Doctrine, prime and basic teaching of spiritual truth, is vital to understanding "the faith once and for all delivered unto the saints."

A doctrine is therefore one of the principal teachings of the Bible, particularly a fundamental truth, essential for soundness and orthodoxy.

Forms of doctrine
Old Testament doctrine
In the Scriptures are doctrinal teachings peculiar to the Old Testament and to the Dispensation of Law. The whole Law of Moses contains the doctrinal teachings that were to guide and govern the life, the lifestyle and the total economy of Israel. Behind the literal interpretation, timeless principles abide that are applicable to all. Types prefigure New Testament realities.

Jewish doctrine
Adding to the Torah, Jewish teachers such as the Pharisees and the Sadducees developed traditions that practically equaled and sometimes superceded revealed Old Testament truth. This Jesus soundly condemned.

New Testament doctrine
The accumulated, revealed truths in the New Testament about God, Christ, the Holy Spirit, the atonement, the Church, the second coming of

Christ and many more, build upon and interpret the doctrines revealed in the Old Testament. Christ introduced a new covenant, a new dispensation, a new era. None of His teachings do away with the timeless truth in the Old Testament. Sacrifices are seen to be symbols of Christ's one and final sacrifice. The book of Galatians well explains the new Age of Grace.

Christological doctrine

So important is Christ that all Scripture is really a revelation of Him, directly or indirectly. Only New Testament believers can see the reality of this truth.

False doctrine

Any teaching contrary to the main thrust of Scripture, contradictory to the totality of truth God reveals in His whole Bible on a subject, or something purporting to be a new revelation . . . all come under this category of false doctrine.

Statements of Faith

Baptists and others have sought to systematize, summarize and express the basic doctrines of the Bible in "confessions of faith." Some have adopted the Twenty Articles of Faith, first promulgated in 1923 in the Kansas City meeting of the Baptist Bible Union. Southern Baptists, partially in response to the rise of modernism in their convention, adopted "The Baptist Faith and Message" in 1925, and recently revised it.

Earlier confessions included the New Hampshire Confession of Faith in 1833, The Philadelphia Confession of 1742, and the London Confession of 1689. There are many others. These confessions of faith are important because they set forth the accumulated wisdom of biblical scholars, Bible-preaching pastors and godly theologians who have preceded us.

Study your church's Confession of Faith, looking up the Scriptures appended thereto. Learn what you share doctrinally with a whole body of believers.

These are the major doctrines.

Studying a Bible doctrine

Now, you need to do some diligent studying of Bible doctrines on your own so you may know of a surety just what you believe.

Research the Scriptures on the subject.

Here you can use your concordance and your topical Bible. If you are going to study the doctrine of the Holy Spirit, for instance, look up all the references to the Spirit in the Old and New Testaments in a concordance. A shortcut is to turn to your topical Bible and look up "Holy Spirit." Read all the verses.

Observe the progress of the doctrine.

Remember the law of Progressive Mention. "From the first mention of a subject to the last mention, there is a progress of doctrine, yet the first mention and the last mention indicate what is between, and the intermediate matter is found to be fitly joined together."

Compare the doctrine with balancing truths.

When studying repentance, also consider its counterpart, saving faith. When election is considered, look at the free will of man, too. Contrast the New Covenant with the Old Covenant. Emphasize the ideas that the Bible stresses. Christ, salvation and Christian living are all themes with much emphasis.

Express the doctrine in simplicity.

Write down a definition of each truth you study. Avoid pedantic and heavy theological terms. When a profound idea is set forth in easily understood language, great communication takes place.

Practice what you believe.

To be doctrinally correct and be in practice a poor Christian is a travesty on truth.

Use your study tools.

One of your ten basic tools for Bible study is a Bible doctrine compendium. Here are some suggestions:

- *What the Faith is All About*, by Elmer Towns, vice president of Liberty University, is an excellent help in popular language, a simplified "systematic theology" almost anyone can use. Some 52 doctrines are covered.

- *All the Doctrines of the Bible*, by Herbert Lockyer, expounds some 31 major doctrinal concepts.

- *What the Bible Teaches*, by R. A. Torrey, is an older work which consists primarily of Scripture arranged under theological or doctrinal headings, followed by propositions and conclusions. It is still in print and a most valuable aid.

- *Bancroft's Christian Theology and Elemental Theology* are somewhat more advanced studies, useful for preachers and teachers.

There are many other fine volumes and a vast reservoir of theological tomes in libraries for those who want to gain degrees in the field.

The above listed volumes are for anyone.

Study for yourself

Make up a list of doctrines you want to consider, and with the use of the tools suggested, dig into them.

Do not neglect your Articles of Faith or Confession. Study them carefully. They are the product of centuries of study.

Always make notes, unless you have an infallible memory and a photographic mind.

Make up a whole notebook on Bible doctrines for your own use.

Do not imagine that you are going to get a "new doctrine" or a "new revelation." You may see some new aspects of truth, but God is not originating new major doctrines.

In this era of spiritual compromise, it is more important than ever to know what the Bible teaches, what you believe, and then to take your stand for the fundamentals.

DOCTRINE. In the Old Testament, the word occurs chiefly as a translation of *leqah*, meaning 'what is received' (Dt. 32:2; Jb. 6: 4; Pr. 4:2; Is. 29:24). The idea of a body of revealed teaching is chiefly expressed by *tora*, which occurs 216 times and is rendered as 'law.'

In the New Testament two words are used, *Didaskalia* means both act and the content of teaching. It is used of the Pharisees' teaching (Mt. 15:9; Mk. 7:7). Apart from one instance in Colossians and one in Ephesians, it is otherwise confined to the Pastoral Epistles (and seems to refer often to some body of teaching used as a standard of orthodoxy). *Didache* is used in more parts of the New Testament. It too can mean either the act or the content of teaching. It occurs of the teaching of Jesus (Mt. 7:28, etc) which He claimed to be divine (Jn. 7:16, 17). After Pentecost Christian doctrine began to be formulated (Acts 2:42) as the instruction given to those who had responded to the *kerygma* (Rom 6:17). There were some in the Church whose official function was to teach this to new converts (e.g. 1 Cor. 11:28, 29).

–from *The New Bible Dictionary*, J. D. Douglas (editor),
Wm. B. Eerdmans Publishing Co., Grand Rapids, Michigan

But God be thanked, that ye were the servants of sin, but ye have obeyed from the heart that form of doctrine which was delivered you (Romans 6:17).

BIBLICAL DISPENSATIONS

Eternity Past — Eternity Future

Key events across the top: Law Fulfilled Matt. 27:50–51 · Rapture of Saved 1 Thess. 4:16–17 · Return of Christ in Glory Rev. 19:11–16 · White Throne · Lake of Fire · 7 Years Tribulation

	Innocence	Conscience	Human Government	Promise	Law	Church Age	Millennial Reign
Event	Creation	The Fall	The Flood	Tower of Babel	Exodus	Dispersion of Israel Ezek. 36:16–19 / Regathering of Israel Ezek. 36:20–24	Armageddon
Responsibility	Obey God Gen. 1:26–28; 2:15–17	Do Good, Blood Sacrifice Gen. 3:5, 7, 22; 4:4	Scatter and Multiply Gen. 8:15—9:7	Dwell in Canaan Gen. 12:1–7	Keep the Whole Law Ex. 19:3–8	Faith in Jesus, Keep Doctrine Pure John 1:12; Rom. 8:1–4; Eph. 2:8–9	Obey and Worship Jesus Isa. 11:3–5; Zech. 14:9, 16
Failure	Disobedience Gen. 3:1–6	Wickedness Gen 6:5–6, 11–12	Did Not Scatter Gen. 11:1–4	Dwelt in Egypt Gen. 12:10; 46:6	Broke Law 2 Kgs. 17:7–20; Matt. 27:1–25	Impure Doctrine John 5:39–40; 2 Tim. 3:1–7	Final Rebellion Rev. 20:7–9
Judgment	Curse and Death Gen. 3:7–19	Flood Gen. 6:7, 13; 7:11–14	Confusion of Languages Gen. 11:5–9	Egyptian Bondage Ex. 1:8–14	Worldwide Dispersion Deut. 28:63–66; Luke 21:20–24	Apostasy, False Doctrine 2 Thess. 2:3; 2 Tim. 4:3	Satan Loosed, Eternal Hell Rev. 20:11–15

Israel (Promise, Law)

14

HOW TO STUDY DISPENSATIONS

How strange it is that a subject like *dispensations* should arouse such determined antipathy and insistent opposition among some who claim to believe the inerrant Word of God, or who otherwise positionalize themselves as fundamentalists or conservatives!

Erroneous assertions are rife in theological circles, with a frequent claim that Englishman J. N. Darby in the 1830's invented the whole idea of distinctive time periods in the history of God's progressive revelation of Himself over the whole scope of human habitation on this planet. This blatant error must be disproved, a relatively easy task for the unbiased.

In his classic work, *Dispensationalism Today*, Charles C. Ryrie has presented powerful evidence all the way from postapostolic times that the concept of eras, periods of different dealings with humanity, and progressive development of biblical history in discernable epochs have always been a part of Christian theology. No serious Bible student should be without this valuable tool.

It is true that the widespread understanding of dispensationalism was sparked in the 19th century by many students and scholars, of which J. N. Darby was one, and Baptist writer James R. Graves was another. The publication and popularization of the Scofield Reference Bible has brought these concepts to the average Bible-reading Christian, as have other popular writings based on a basically literal interpretation of Scripture.

Often, a critic will select the poorest example of dispensational thought, perhaps even an ultra-dispensational viewpoint, and then equate it with all dispensational interpretation.

We were taught in psychology classes that this comes under the heading of "cloudy thinking."

What a dispensation is

Scofield says, "A dispensation is a period of time during which man is tested in respect to some specific revelation of the will of God."

Ryrie approaches the concept from a different stance, emphasizing less the time factor and more the idea that a dispensation is an "economy" from the Greek word *oikonomia* (translated dispensation, stewardship, etc.), a method of management or administration. "A dispensation is a distinguishable economy in the outworking of God's purpose," he states.

Ironside, the prolific writer, defined a dispensation as "an economy . . . an ordered condition of things . . . There are various *economies* running through the Word of God. A dispensation, an economy, then, is that particular order or condition of things prevailing in one age which does not necessarily prevail in another."

Dispensationalists *do not teach*, as some writers have recently erred in reporting, that there are different methods of salvation or "multiple plans of salvation." That is incorrect.

The real issue is hermeneutics

Dispensationalists believe the Scriptures should be interpreted normally and literally, giving ample allowances for obvious figures of speech, typical meanings, and practical applications, but never negating the basic literal significance of a passage.

"When the plain sense of Scripture makes common sense, seek no other sense . . ." It is very evident that the Bible describes a succession of different periods in the history of His dealing with the human race from Adam to Christ. The dispensationalist recognizes pivotal events of biblical history and simply systemizes the changed conditions that results. These include the Fall of man, the Flood, post-Deluge Civilization, the call of Abraham, and the Giving of the Law.

How many dispensations?

While these writers will be charged with being too simplistic, we are bold to say that nobody can understand the Bible at all without being at least an elementary dispensationalist. To distinguish between the Old Testament era and the dealings of God, particularly with the Jews and the New Testament era in which Christianity is offered to the world, is absolutely essential to understanding the Bible. Are these two epochs in history not "dispensations" in the classic sense of the word? Of course they are, notwithstanding the prejudiced objections of anti-dispensationalists.

Most responsible followers of dispensational theology add to these two basic "economies" a literal millennium or kingdom age, basing that interpretation on the natural meaning of Old Testament prophecies of the future golden age for Israel and the world and the frequent references by New Testament writers to the future reign of Christ.

These three dispensations: that of Law, or Legal Dispensation; Grace or that of Gospel Dispensation; and the Kingdom or Millennial Dispensation . . . are prominent, clearly-defined time periods so evident to the simple or profound pursuit of truth that it seems absurd to have to defend the concepts at all.

Often a critic will select the poorest example of dispensational thought, perhaps even an ultra-dispensational viewpoint, and then equate it with all dispensational interpretation.

Again, willing to be accused of simplicity, I see it as obvious that God's dealings with Adam and Eve before the Fall differed from His dealings after the Fall. Likewise, the *antediluvian* era is presented in a different light from the *postdiluvian* era or "the Age of the Patriarchs."

But even a scholar, considering all of ancient biblical history as progressive rather than epochal, has to admit that this giving of the Law, the Exodus, and the rise of the Hebrew nation in Sinai are theological and historical hinges on which subsequent Old Testament revelation swings.

Most dispensationalists recognize SEVEN DISPENSATIONS:

First, the Dispensation of Innocence, or the Adamic Dispensation, the period of human history prior to the Fall (Genesis 1-3).

Second, the Dispensation of Conscience, or the Antediluvian Dispensation, stretching from the Fall to the flood (Genesis 3-8).

Third, the Dispensation of Human Government, or the Postdiluvian

Dispensation, beginning with the Flood, including the tower of Babel crisis, and closing with the call of Abraham (Genesis 8-11).

Fourth, the Dispensation of Promise or the Patriarchal Dispensation, commencing with Abraham and terminating at Sinai with the giving of the Law. Paul in Galatians distinguishes between an age of "promise" and the age of "law" (Genesis 12-Exodus 19).

Fifth, the Dispensation of Law, or the Israelite/Jewish Dispensation, inaugurated at Sinai and terminated by Christ's death and resurrection when He became "the end of the law" for righteousness to everyone that believeth (Exodus 19-Matthew 27-28; Mark 16; Luke 23-24; John 1:11, 19-25; Acts 1:2).

Sixth, the Dispensation of Grace or the Gospel Dispensation, launched at the resurrection and continuing (through a transition period in New Testament times) until today. The prophesied Great Tribulation period will mark its close (Acts 1:2-The Return of Christ-Revelation 19).

Seventh, the Dispensation of the Kingdom or the Millennial "Economy" Dispensation when Christ will fulfill Old and New Testament prophecies concerning Israel and the world in a glorious reign of peace on this earth. Christ indicated that the twelve apostles would indeed sit on twelve thrones, judging the twelve tribes of Israel (Matthew 19:8; Revelation 22).

Each "economy" begins with a vital revelation of truth and ends with a judgment on mankind for failure to fully accept truth. Study these in detail, making notes on special characteristics of each dispensation, including comparisons and contrasts.

A simple chart, either one of those in circulation or that which you compose yourself, will assist you in seeing biblical history.

Where did dispensationalism begin?

Originally, Paul used the expression "dispensation of the grace of God" in Ephesians 3:2 to indicate his stewardship of the message of grace which he then introduced to the world. This has become an ongoing process. Again he alludes to the "dispensation of the fullness of time" in Ephesians 1:10, which seems to indicate a future glorious consummation under Christ.

Seed ideas among church fathers

According to Charles Ryrie, Justin Martyr (110-165) alludes to different programs of God in history and spoke of the present "dispensation." Irenaeus (130-200) describes different time periods during which God dealt differently with humans and spoke of the "Christian dispensation."

Discussing Old Testament times, Augustine in the 5th century wrote, "The divine institution of sacrifice was suitable in the former dispensation, but is not suitable now . . ."

No one asserts that these early church fathers were "dispensationalists" in the contemporary sense, but certainly the root ideas are evident in their writings.

Since the Reformation

In 1687, A French philosopher, Pierre Poiret, published his work, *L'O Economie Divine*, which contained a system of seven dispensations, slightly different from the generally-accepted series.

John Edwards, cited by Ryrie, published a two-volume work in 1699 entitled *A Competent History or Survey of All the Dispensations*.

Isaac Watts, in the 1700's, better known for his hymns, was also a prolific theological writer. In a 40-page essay entitled "The Harmony of All the Religions which God ever Prescribed in Men and all his Dispensations toward them," he sets forth a basic system of dispensations, very similar to that which Scofield advocated, with the exception of the millennium, which he did not consider to be a dispensation.

In 1883, J. R. Graves, the great 19th Century Baptist theologian and leader of the Landmark movement, published a book, still in print, entitled, *The Work of Christ in Seven Dispensations*, the product of a lifetime of study, in which he sets forth the basic seven dispensations, varying only slightly from Watts and the later-published Scofield Bible. Graves taught a pre-tribulational rapture, a literal restoration of Israel, and a glorious millennium on earth. The oft-repeated assertion that dispensationalism is not a part of Baptist theology or history is completely erroneous. Graves was a Southern Baptist all of his life and ministry. During the late 19th century, Englishman John Nelson Darby, a prolific writer, advanced and popularized dispensational thought in Europe and America.

A sensible approach to dispensational truth

Any truth can be warped beyond its intended purpose, and no thinking believer wants to divide up the Scriptures in such an absurd fashion that such treasures as the synoptic Gospels are consigned to some mini-dispensation, and therefore not applicable to present-day living. "All Scripture . . . is profitable for doctrine . . ."

Avoid extremist views held by an elitist minority who claim they alone have truth. On the other hand, the denial of dispensational concepts is just as likely to lead to strange spiritualizing of obviously prophetic and literal passages. Some theologians have written such totally inaccurate interpretations of dispensationalism that it seems they scarcely have researched the whole subject.

Study the dispensations, particularly the major previously mentioned three, allowing some latitude for variation of opinions on the earlier eras of human history as revealed in Scripture. If you have any artistic skills, plan your own chart.

It is very interesting that no dispensationalist ever becomes a modernist (unless he discards his dispensational convictions). Dispensationalists have been among the strongest advocates of world missions.

---

1 For this cause I Paul, the prisoner of Jesus Christ for you Gentiles, 2 If ye have heard of the dispensation of the grace of God which is given me to you-ward: 3 How that by revelation he made known unto me the mystery; (as I wrote afore in few words, 4 Whereby, when ye read, ye may understand my knowledge in the mystery of Christ)(Ephesians 3:1-2)

9 Having made known unto us the mystery of his will, according to his good pleasure which he hath purposed in himself: 10 That in the dispensation of the fullness of times he might gather together in one all things in Christ, both which are in heaven, and which are on earth; [even] in him: (Ephesians 1:9-10)

15

HOW TO STUDY BIBLE COVENANTS

Many professing biblical conservatives follow a line of interpretation known as *Covenant Theology*. This viewpoint spiritualizes Old Testament promises and provisions made for Israel, basing all of God's purposes and undertakings upon His one *attribute of grace*, and applying both the letter (in some cases) and the spirit of Old Testament conditional and unconditional promises to New Testament Christians. Covenant theologians often see Israel as an "Old Testament church" and Christians as the believing "remnant" entitled to blessings, while Israel inherits the cursings for disobedience.

Covenant Theology scoffs at Dispensational Theology and perceives only one overall plan of God for a people. Israel as a nation is relegated to history. This one covenant of grace idea arose in the 17th century, popularized by John Colceius (1603-1669).

Dispensational Theology, which does not teach multiple plans of salvation, emphasizes that Israel has never been the Church, is not the Church now, and will never be "The Church." Dispensationalists, following a basically literalist (and obvious) interpretation of Scripture, believe that Israel is Israel in the past and in the future. That Israel is distinct from the family of God in this age seems so crystal clear from the reading of the Word that defending that viewpoint should not even be necessary. Unfortunately, it is.

But, that there are "covenants" between God and man, God and Israel, and God and believers today is a truth worthy of exploration.

A Bible covenant is an agreement God initiates with human beings, either with or without conditions, assuring that God will perform certain acts and provide certain blessings for them.

At least eight covenants are revealed in Scripture, the study of which will enable the serious scholar to interpret God's dealings with the whole human race, the nation of Israel and the people of God in this age.

The Edenic Covenant

Prior to the Fall, God spoke to His newly-created pair, Adam and Eve (Genesis 1:26-31), bestowing the leadership of the earth upon them, but also placing a single restriction, a test of obedience, upon them (Genesis 2:15-17). The first part of the covenant was unconditional, but residence in the perfect environment in Eden was conditional. Man failed.

The Adamic Covenant

Following Adam's transgression, God set forth the conditions of life for man, conditions that remain unto this day (Genesis 3:14-19). God promises that "the woman's seed" will bruise the serpent's head in His address to Satan (verse 15). His message to Eve (verse 16) and his message to Adam (verse 17) should be carefully studied.

The Noahic Covenant

As the flood waters receded and Noah and his family were atop Mount Ararat (sole survivors of the great inundation), God blessed Noah and established His covenant with him and his descendants (Genesis 8:20-22; 9:1-17). Careful consideration of these promises enables us to understand the ongoing of history as we have known it. No special conditions which man must meet are here, either.

The Abrahamic Covenant

Nearly 4,000 years ago God sovereignly selected Abraham as the great progenitor of His earthly-chosen people, the ancestor of Christ (humanly speaking), the one through whom all nations of the earth would be blessed. (Study Genesis 12:1-4; 13:14-17; 15:1-7; 17:1-8).

The promise of blessing upon His descendents (Israelites and Ishmaelites) does not include the believers of this age, too. According to Paul in Galatians 4 and 5 we are the spiritual seed of Abraham by faith. Christians are never called the New Israel, since we are Abraham's spiritual seed or descendants through faith in Christ who was likewise a descendant of Abraham.

The Mosaic Covenant

Thirty-five centuries ago, the Lord used Moses to emancipate His earthly-chosen people who had become a great nation of two million. At the foot of Sinai, they encamped while Moses at the summit received the Laws of God. Then the Lord established a covenant with His people Israel, involving various conditions which, if followed, would assure blessings. This is the "First Covenant" discussed in Hebrews 9, which has been supplanted in the Dispensation of Grace by the New Covenant (Testament). Carefully research Exodus 10:1-16; 21:1-24:11, and 31:18. This covenant, like the Abrahamic, was for the people of Israel, although principles of righteousness and truth, explained and amplified in the New Testament from Old Testament Scriptures, are timeless and transcend all ages and dispensations. Studying Hebrews 6-10 brings out the contrasts between the Abrahamic Covenant and Mosaic Covenant compared with the New Covenant Christ has introduced.

A Bible covenant is an agreement God initiates with human beings, either with or without conditions, assuring that God will perform certain acts and provide certain blessings for them.

The Land Covenant

Again, this relates to the nation of Israel and their descendants and the promised land. "The territory they could occupy and enjoy." It is a conditional covenant which was given by God to the new generation of Israelites who were about to enter the promised land. This has never been abrogated and will come to full fruition in the millennium (Deuteronomy 30 and Ezekiel 40-48).

The Davidic Covenant

A thousand years before Christ, God made this agreement with David, guaranteeing the perpetuity of his dynasty. One condition was imposed. If a royal descendent disobeyed the Lord, he would suffer chastisement, but the covenant would never be abrogated. The royal Davidic line of kings continued until 586 B.C. and the destruction of Jerusalem. Matthew 1 presents the royal family's heirs to the throne, culminating in Christ, who is (humanly speaking) of the seed of David and who has the right to reign over Israel. That right He will yet exercise when He comes into His kingdom and rules with the 12 apostles over Israel (Matthew 19:27,28).

Peruse the contents of 2 Samuel 7 for the wording of this covenant, conveyed through the prophet Nathan.

The New Covenant

When Christ said, "This is the New Testament (Covenant) in my blood; drink ye all of it," He began the establishment of the prophesied (Jeremiah 31:31-37) New Covenant which involved His sacrificial ministry, His fulfillment of the Old Testament types, and introduction of the new and living way to God through Christ, symbolically revealed in the Old Covenant. The words "Testament" and "Covenant" are the same in the Greek language (*diatheke*).

We believers enjoy the spiritual benefits of this New Covenant.

In the millennium, the Israelites will enter into the spiritual and temporal blessings brought about by the First and Second Advents of Christ our Lord, included in this New Covenant (Jeremiah 31).

An easily accessible and understandable presentation of these eight covenants can be found in your Scofield Reference Bible, although he certainly is not the originator of these concepts.

The first three relate to the entire human race. The next four are directly relevant to Israel. The New Covenant, the eighth, is for Christians today and for the converted Jews of the Kingdom Age who will revere Jesus as their Messiah-King, as so lucidly depicted in the Word of God.

In searching the Scriptures for yourself and gaining a comprehensive understanding of the Word of God, do not neglect the covenants.

Some suggestions for research

- Look up all the covenants in the referenced passages and read the promises and conditions, if any.

- Use a page or more for your notes on each covenant.

- Write out the name and definition of each covenant at the top of the page.

- Number and list the promises.

- List the conditions, if any.

- Remember that promises to Israel and David are precisely that. There is no room for spiritualizing away the obvious meaning of these passages.

- With the New Covenant, careful comparison of the Jeremiah passages, the gospel account of the institution of the Lord's Supper (Mark 14:22-25; 1 Corinthians 11:23-26) and Hebrews 8-10, is vital to understanding the contrast between the Old Testament and the New Testament.

- Look up the marginal references in all of the above passages.

- Study how the New Covenant applies to Jews and Gentiles today and how it will be applied in the future millennial age.

- If you have a *Scofield Reference Bible*, a *Tim LaHaye Prophecy Study Bible* or a *John Hagee Prophecy Bible*, read all of their notes on the covenants. Copy them on a notepad. This will help you master this interesting field of biblical investigation.

- Compare the covenants with the dispensations to further "rightly divide the Word of truth."

But now hath he obtained a more excellent ministry, by how much also he is the mediator of a better covenant, which was established upon better promises. For if that first [covenant] had been faultless, then should no place have been sought for the second (Hebrews 8:6, 7).

The Unconditional **New Covenant** fulfills the redemptive conditions envisioned by the conditional old Mosaic Covenant. Originally promised to Israel (Jer. 32; Ezek. 11, 36), this covenant extended salvation to the Gentiles through Christ, the Messenger and Mediator of a better covenant purchased with His own blood. In this covenant, through Christ, believers receive:

1. Grace (Heb. 10:29)
2. Peace (Isa. 54:10; Ezek. 34:25; 37:26)
3. Spirit of God (Isa. 59:21)
4. Redemption (Isa. 49:8; Jer 31:34; Heb. 10:19-20)
5. Removal of sin (Jer. 31:34, Rom. 11:27; Heb. 10:17)
6. New heart (Jer. 31:33; Heb. 8:10; 10:16)
7. New relationship with God
             (Jer. 31:33; Ezek. 16:62; 37:26-27; Heb. 8:10).

–Richard Mayhue

16

HOW TO STUDY BIBLE POETRY

Commonly, the books of Job, Psalms, Proverbs, Ecclesiastes and Song of Solomon are known as "the Poetical Books."

The Jews, however, regarded only the first three as a poetical section, since Ecclesiastes is more of an eloquent sermon in both expositional and poetical form. The Song of Solomon is obviously poetry, but placed in the Hebrew canon with Ruth, Lamentations, Ecclesiastes and Esther in a separate group.

Lamentations is also a poetical composition.

Nor are we to suppose that this is all the poetry in the Bible. The Song of Moses and Miriam (Exodus 15:1-21); the Song of Deborah and Barak (Judges 5); the Song of David at Saul and Jonathan's death (2 Samuel 1:19-27); and David's Song of Deliverance (2 Samuel 22) are some of the major poetical passages in the earlier books of the Bible.

In the book of Isaiah, who was the John Milton of his time, there are long passages of eloquent prophecies that are so beautifully stated that it sounds and reads like poetry. That is true of some other prophets.

Of course, Bible poetry, like Bible prose, is inspired of God and contains truth without any admixture of error.

Obvious figurative expressions like Psalm 104:3 are poetic, and are not to be taken in a direct literal sense:

"Who maketh the clouds his chariot."

"Who walketh upon the wings of the wind."

There are thousands of such metaphors, similes, personifications and other plain and obvious poetic figures of speech in the Bible.

While we advocate taking the Bible for what it says, we do not literalize obvious figurative language.

Nor are we of the group who would turn plain, literal narratives or historical accounts or spiritual teaching into farfetched allegories, symbols, or some meaning foreign to the context or content of a passage. It is a mistake to try to spiritualize what is actual history or direct teaching. This in no way precludes application of spiritual principles in our lives (1 Cor. 10:4).

Distinctives of Hebrew Poetry

Since the Old Testament was written in Hebrew between 1400 and 400 B.C., it is necessary to note the distinctives of Hebrew poetry.

Hebrew poetry does not rhyme, as does most English poetry. Nor does it have the same kind of meter or rhythm that English poetry has.

Shakespeare, for instance, seldom wrote in rhyme, but his plays are written in lines with five beats or emphases per line. This is known as iambic pentameter. Much of his writing is beautiful, eloquent poetry, although it tells stories based on actual historical events in dramatized form.

Hebrew poetry contains a "rhyming" of ideas.

This is sometimes called "parallelism." That is, one line contains an idea that is "paralleled," or expressed differently and further in the next line. Two such lines usually constituted a verse. Remember that verse divisions were not made until the 15th century.

Look for three kinds of "parallelism" when reading Job, Psalms and Proverbs:

Completive (sometimes called synonymous).

Here an idea is presented in one line (or the first half of a verse) and expanded with a similar idea in the next line (second half of a verse).

Here is an example from Psalm 83:1

    a.   *Keep not thou silence, O God:*
    b.   *Hold not thy peace, and be not still, O God.*

Observe that line b expresses a similar idea as line a, but expands upon it and completes the thought.

Here is another case:

a. *Hear this, all ye people,*

b. *Give ear, all ye inhabitants of the world* (Psalm 49:1).

Again, notice that the ideas are similar, but not quite exactly the same.
The second line completes the thought of the first line.

There are thousands of cases like this in the poetical books.

Constrastive (sometimes called antithetical).

Instead of a similar idea in the second line, there is an opposing or contrasting idea.

Look at these examples:

a. *A merry heart maketh a cheerful countenance:*

b. *But by sorrow of heart the spirit is broken* (Proverbs 15:13).

Two attitudes of the heart and two results are compared.
Another example:

a. *The wicked worketh a deceitful work:*

b. *But to him that soweth righteousness shall be a sure reward*
    (Proverbs 11:18).

Often there is this contrast between the righteous and the wicked in
Psalms and Proverbs. Look for the English word "but," linking the contrasts.

Constructive (sometimes called synthetic or progressive).

In this form of parallelism, the second line expands and builds on the idea
in the first line, often presenting the result of complying with the teaching
of the first line.

Watch for the English words "and" and "for" in the middle of the verse.

a. *A man's gift maketh room for him*

b. *And bringeth him before great men"* (Proverbs 16:18).

Consider this progression of truth:

a.   *Keep thy heart with all diligence;*

b.   *For out of it are the issues of life* (Proverbs 4:23).

There are all kinds of variations of these basic forms. You will find double sets of contrastive parallels, even triple sets. Look up Isaiah 45:13, and mark the three "Beholds," each initiating a contrast.

Scholars sometimes refer to a two-line parallel as a *distich*, a three-line as a *tristich*, a four-line as a *tetratich*. I do not know why, unless they want to sound scholarly or believe "a stitch in time saves nine."

The value of acrostics and alliteration

Hebrew poetry also employed alphabetical arrangements as an aid to memory, since many of the compositions were sung or recited publicly, and were therefore memorized.

Psalm 119

Turn to Psalm 119 as a major illustration.

Here you have 22 sections in this great sonnet, extolling the Word of God. Each section is headed by a Hebrew letter. Your King James translation has the Hebrew letter in original form, plus an Anglicized spelling of the letter to aid you in pronunciation.

The eight verses under ALEPH all begin with the letter ALEPH (equivalent to English A) in Hebrew. Therefore, you have an alliteration of "A"s appearing 8 times, the first word starting with ALEPH.

The second eight verses begin with BETH (B) in Hebrew. Each first word starts with BETH (B). These alliterations are not translatable into English or any other language, of course.

You go all the way through the 22-letter Hebrew alphabet in order with the same pattern, each set of 8 verses starting with a word beginning with the same letter. You can see how easy it would be to memorize and sing. Study this Psalm and learn the Hebrew alphabet. It is right there in your Bible.

All the alphabetical Psalms include chapter 25, 34, 111, 112, 119 and 145.

The Book of Lamentations

The four chapters are arranged in acrostic form. The first two chapters and the last two contain 22 verses, the first word of every verse in the Hebrew language begins with a letter of the Hebrew alphabet, beginning with ALEPH (A), verse one, and continuing through TAU (T), the last letter of their alphabet, verse twenty-two.

The middle chapter, with 66 verses, has the first three verses starting with a word beginning with ALEPH (A); the second three verses begin with words starting with BETH (B), and so on, through the Hebrew alphabet.

We have used the letters in Psalm 119 to mark the verses in my Bible ALEPH through TAU through the first four chapters of Lamentations. The last chapter contains 22 verses but is not in acrostic format.

Proverbs 31:10-31

These 22 verses that describe the ideal woman are in the Hebrew set forth in acrostic form, each verse beginning with a word starting with a letter of the Hebrew alphabet, ALEPH through TAU.

Other characteristics of Hebrew poetry

Many of these psalms were chanted or sung with a certain rhythm, which may have involved a kind of meter or singsong repetition of long and short notes. Not having Choirmaster Asaph to consult (he died three thousand years ago), we have no way of knowing exactly how the Hebrews sounded when singing. There were orchestras (Psalm 150), to be sure.

Divinely inspired as the words were and are, all of these great poetic compositions contain truth and teaching for our learning and admonition.

Because Hebrew poetry did not rhyme, and how it was sung originally is not fully known, it is wonderfully suitable for translation into any language.

Commonly, the books of Job, Psalms, Proverbs, Ecclesiastes and Song of Solomon are known as "the Poetical Books."

Rhymed English (or Spanish, or any other language) poetry is very difficult to translate, since all languages have different-sounding words and different-length words for the same idea. Therefore, both rhyme and meter are lost in translation.

But the ideas expressed in these words can be translated into the words of any language, perfectly preserving the parallelism. Its beauty, force and sense is undiminished.

Using these truths

While counted generally as a poetic book, Ecclesiastes is also a sermon. Great speakers like Solomon, Isaiah and Hosea preached and taught with this marvelous flow of language, often in poetic form. If you have a flair for expressing yourself in poetic form, use it for the glory of God.

Some suggestions for research

- Read these books with marking pencil in hand.Note again the punctuation, the "buts," the "ands" and the "fors." Mark them.

- Look for repeated verses which constituted a chorus that a congregation might sing in response. Psalm 136, for instance, contains the refrain, "for his mercy endureth forever" as the last half of every verse. The song leader probably sang the first half, and the congregation responded by singing "for his mercy endureth forever." Not many people could read and write in those days. They needed lots of help in public worship.

- Study repeated words, like in Psalm 103:2-5, in which there are five "WHOs." Note the "BLESSEDs" and "BLESS." Study Psalm 1 in detail for illustrations of parallelism.

- In studying and preaching, these divinely-designed poetic forms make great points for sermons and meditation.

- In the Psalms, look for the Messianic psalms predicting Christ; the millennial psalms prophesying the golden age; the prayer psalms; the praise psalms, the historical psalms, always singing in your own heart. If you find it, buy Arno Gaebelein's book on the Psalms.

- Remember that Lamentations was written by Jeremiah and has been called an "elegy composed in a graveyard." These were the sad songs of Jeremiah when the defeated Israelites were under the heel of the conquering Babylonians. Yet, find the note of hope for Israel in the future.

- Study Old Testament poetry in the prophetic books. Most of the Old Testament prophets wrote their messages in both narrative and poetic forms. These include Isaiah, Jeremiah, Hosea, Joel, Amos, Obadiah, Micah, Nahum, Habakkuk, Zephaniah, and Malachi. Some additions of the Bible differentiate between narrative and poetry by arranging the poetic sections into the appropriate style, thus making it easier to recognize.

- With reverence for the Word of God, enthusiasm for His service, and a heart filled with praise, study these poetical works, resolving to learn and practice the godly life.

Herbert Lockyer's book *All the Poetry of the Bible* is an excellent tool for indepth study (Zondervan Publishers).

POETIC WORSHIP

Nowhere is the genius of Hebrew poetry more apparent than in its imagery. It lays heaven and earth under tribute. It steals music from the morning stars and light from the bridegroom who needs no virginal lamps. Its eternal summer fades not, and its snows are undefiled. It rules the raging of the sea, it drives on the clouds and rides on the wings of the wind. It makes the royal gold richer, the myrrh more fragrant, and the frankincense sweeter. The offerings it takes from the shepherd suffer no death, and his flock is folded in evergreen pastures. The bread of its harvest will never waste, the oil from its press never fail, and its wine is forever new. So long as men can breathe, its eternal lines will form the litany of the praying heart. The strings it touches are the strings of the harp of God.

The rhythm of Hebrew poetry is not the measured beat of the earth-locked body. It is the majestic rhythm of the soaring spirit, felt only by him who has the music of heaven in his soul. It rises above the metrical to a loftier plane and to a new dimension—the dimension of the spirit, where they who worship God worship Him in spirit and truth.

–W. J. M.

17

How to Begin Simple Greek/Hebrew Word Studies

When holy men of God spake as they were moved by the Holy Ghost, they spoke and wrote in the ancient Hebrew language, and in the New Testament, they spoke and wrote in Koine Greek. Doubtless, God prepared the Greek language, the common and international language of the times, as the right vehicle in which to communicate the verbally (words themselves selected by the Holy Spirit) inspired, inerrant, infallible, plenary Word of God.

Every Greek word written by Matthew, Mark, Luke, John, Paul, James, Peter and Jude, though known perhaps in their own vocabularies, was directly selected and designated by the Holy Spirit.

Some have wondered why the Holy Ghost chose Greek and not Latin, which was also a nearly-universal language. Various reasons have been offered, such as the richness and beauty of Greek being superior to the Romans' tongue, but we simply recognize that it was His choice.

Jesus once said, "Whosoever speaketh a word against the Son of man, it shall be forgiven him: but whosoever speaketh a word against the Holy Ghost, it shall not be forgiven him, neither in this world, neither in the world to come" (Matthew 12:32).

Strange words these . . . for all sins can be forgiven through Christ, can they not? We do not presume to have sufficient wisdom to interpret all that Jesus may have implied here.

One thing is sure. We have no intention of "speaking a word against the Holy Ghost" for inspiring the New Testament in Greek. His direct inspiration of the Word of God in Hebrew and Greek has to be His greatest work and ministry.

To "speak a word against the Holy Ghost," downgrading His ministry in inspiring the original autographs penned by the human writers in

His chosen languages would be a course of folly in my judgment, too close to a violation of one of Christ's strongest prohibitions with the severest penalty imaginable. We dare not speak against the Holy Ghost for inspiring God's Word in Greek!

> *Whosoever speaketh a word against the Holy Ghost, it shall not be forgiven him . . .*

Quite the contrary. It will be edifying to us, though our knowledge of Greek is limited, to avail ourselves of some simple study tools, thus to get into some shades of meaning and into some deeper insights most evident in the original Greek.

It takes a little work, concentration and research. Most of us let our minds get so flabby that intellectual laziness may prevent us from investigating the riches of God's truth with diligence and zeal.

Here are some tools that any of us with or without Greek language expertise can use. It will take a few dollars investment, but the rich rewards of increased Bible knowledge and understanding cannot be measured monetarily.

BERRY'S INTERLINEAR

Jim bought his first *Interlinear Greek New Testament* text in 1944, prepared by George Ricker Berry, Ph.D. The Greek test he uses is, of course, "the Textus Receptus," the culmination of the Eastern Byzantine Greek text, divinely preserved and carefully copied by Greek Orthodox clergy and scholars for a thousand years.

The term "Textus Receptus" or "Received Text" was first used in 1624 in an edition published by the Elzivia Brothers, but is essentially the same as the Erasmus-Stephens text of A.D. 1550.

This text is the direct descendent of the text compiled and completed by Lucian of Antioch, founder of the first theological seminary in history about A.D. 280 Lucian may have had copies of originals at his disposal. His work developed into the Byzantine text type, which acquired prominence in the Eastern church and continued to be the current text throughout the middle ages, being the basis for the work of Erasmus and Stephanus 500 years ago. From this text type the English translations of the 16th century were made, culminating in the King James translation in the 17th century.

Berry's interlinear contains the Greek text with an English-equivalent word directly beneath it and the King James translation in the margin. It is a very valuable tool with a lexicon in the back which aids in looking up the various meanings of the original Holy Spirit-inspired Greek words.

STRONG'S OR YOUNG'S CONCORDANCE

Both of these concordances have varying meanings for the original Greek words, aiding in the proper understanding of Scripture. With Strong's, there is a number system which can be easily learned but may be cumbersome. Young's Concordance lists the different Greek words that have been translated into English right where you look them up, in English alphabetical order. The great G. Campbell Morgan was once asked about his background for fascinating Greek explanations. "Where did you learn about these Greek words?" an admirer asked. "In Strong's Concordance," came the reply.

This is a valuable tool, but it must be used to be helpful.

VINE'S EXPOSITORY DICTIONARY OF NEW TESTAMENT WORDS

Alphabetically arranged in English words, this 1,300-page resource book is an invaluable tool. The Greek words under the English word are spelled in English letters, somewhat phonetically, and the word also appears in actual Greek letters, making it easy for those of us not really skilled in Greek to pronounce the word. The definitions, shades of meaning, usages, and other information follow.

The significance of this approach is evident with the word FOLLOW. No less than 10 Greek words, each with a slightly different sense, are translated as FOLLOW. Seeing which word is used in a particular case will give insights on the specific and literal meaning of a passage. Thus you study the exact word the Holy Spirit selected.

All of the important words in the New Testament are defined and expounded by W.E. Vine, a great conservative Greek scholar.

OTHER REFERENCE WORKS

Two other recent works might be accorded limited use. Ralph Earle's WORD MEANINGS IN THE NEW TESTAMENT is a chapter by chapter through the New Testament study of significant words in each chapter, keyed to the King James translation. It's almost like a commentary, and contains all Greek words in English letters, spelled phonetically. Like many volumes, study it with a sieve.

Another EXPOSITORY DICTIONARY OF BIBLE WORDS by Lawrence O. Richards, is arranged by subjects, making it more of a study book than a reference volume. It does not give the Greek words in Greek letters, nor the Hebrew words in Hebrew letters, but it does contain a lot of information about Hebrew words. James Strong's and Robert Young's concordances also give Hebrew words and meanings.

THE EXAMPLE OF JOHN 3:16

As an illustration of how to use these tools for deeper understanding of a text, let us look at John 3:16, word for word, and consider each Greek original word and plumb the depths of its meaning.

FOR—*gar*, meaning verily or therefore.

GOD—*theos*, the word from which we get *theology*. The New Testament title for the supreme being. The same word is used in the plural, as in English for other gods.

SO—*outos*, refers to the intensity of love; the word repeats an idea with emphasis. In Greek, the verse begins with this attention-getting expression, this one, this God, this one and no other loved. The idea of *so* is also inherent in the next word.

LOVED—past tense of *agapao*, meaning the deep and constant love and interest of a perfect Being towards entirely-unworthy objects, which ought to produce and foster a reverential love in them towards the Giver.

THE—*ton*, indicating the English *the*, the definite article. Also this, that, one, he, she, it.

WORLD—*kosmos*, signifying primarily order, arrangement, ornament—that is, an orderly-arranged and created world, including the people in it. Our English word *cosmos*, meaning the universe, is derived from the Greek.

THAT—*hoste,* The word means *so, thus, therefore* and precedes what is to be stressed.

HE GAVE—*edoken,* a form of *didomi,* the e includes the idea of *He.* The word means to *give* greatly.

HIS SON—*ton huios,* primarily signifies the relation of an offspring to a parent. John does not use this word for believers, only Christ.

THE ONLY BEGOTTEN—*ton monogene,* one word, the *mono,* meaning only or singly, distinctively, and the form of *gennao,* indicating *birth,* hence, our English words, *generation, generate, progenitor,* etc.

THAT—*hina,* a different word from the previous "that," which was *hoste.* A word specifically typing the previous thought and the following thought close together.

WHOSOEVER—*pas,* meaning anyone (anywhere), everyone with no exceptions. The *o* following in the Greek text means *who.*

BELIEVETH—*pisteuon,* the action verb for the noun *pistis,* which means *faith.* In Greek, *faith* and *believe* are from the same root word. To *believe* is to *have faith* or *exercise faith. Pistis* means a firm persuasion, a conviction based upon hearing (akin to *pietho,* meaning to persuade).

ON—*eis,* which means *on, in, into.*

HIM—*auton.* Note *autou* for *his* earlier in the verse. Our English words beginning with *auto,* meaning *self* or personal, arise from this word, like autobiography.

SHOULD NOT PERISH—*me apoletai,* from *apollumi,* signifying to destroy. The idea is not extinction, but ruin, loss, not of being, but of well-being.

BUT—*holl,* a word that introduces oppositives or contrasts.

HAVE—*ehce*, from *echo*, used with the following meanings: to hold, to hold fast, to cling, to be next to, to possess, to consider, to regard, to own by experience, etc.

EVERLASTING—*aionion*, lasting indefinitely into the *aeons*. Plato used the word for timeless, ideal eternity in which no days or months or years count. The word occurs 17 times in John's Gospel. In the King James, it is translated *eternal* 42 times of the times it occurs in the New Testament.

LIFE—*zoen*, meaning life as a principle, life in the absolute sense, involving a consciousness of its existence. English words *zoo* and *zoology* are derived from the word, indicating living beings and the study of living beings.

This may seem tedious, but there is something wonderful about looking at the exact words chosen by the Holy Ghost, written by the inspired writers, and studying precisely what He said in the Greek language in which He spoke to those holy men of old.

We who treasure the doctrine of *verbal inspiration*, knowing the very words were divinely designated, ought to take time to study those very words from time to time.

Hebrew-Greek Key Word Study Bible
King James Version
Key words in the text numerically coded to James Strong's *Exhaustive Concordance Bible*, Introduction to each book, Exegetical Notes, Center column references, Words of Christ in Red, Grammatical helps to the New Testament, Word Studies, Bible-Concordance, Strong's dictionaries, and color maps.
Executive Editor, Spiros Zodhiates, Th.D.
Managing Editor, Warren Baker, D.R.E.
AMG Publishers
Chattanooga, TN 37422, USA
Available in Bookstores

18

How to Read the Scriptures

Give attendance to reading, to exhortation, to doctrine (1 Timothy 4:13).

It goes without saying that you can never learn the Bible without reading it, rereading it, and familiarizing yourself with it.

There are no shortcuts. You must read.

Read the Bible itself

Select a good Bible with plain print for regular reading. If a giant print Bible suits you, get one. Do not make the mistake of trying to read a tiny print Bible with regularity. You will get discouraged or suffer from eyestrain.

Personally, we read the old *Scofield Reference Bible*, not because of the notes any more, but because we have been looking at the pages for 65 years, with always the same verse on the same place on the same page in every copy. It has been a great help in memorization and for finding a desired verse very quickly.

You may prefer a *Thompson Chain Reference Bible*, a *Ryrie Study Bible*, or any one of a dozen good reference Bibles.

You may just want the simple text of Scripture with no notes at all.

Other study Bibles include: *Dakes' Annotated Reference Bible, The Nelson Study Bible, The Companion Bible, The MacArthur Study Bible*, etc.

When to read

Schedule a special period for reading, probably 20 minutes as a rock-bottom period. Thirty minutes of Bible reading a day will do wonders for your spiritual life. Try early morning or an evening time.

You can carry a pocket Testament and use spare moments to gain wisdom from the Word. Part of a lunch hour, a recess, before dinner, while waiting in a doctor's office or prior to an appointment . . . all such times can be utilized for spiritual profit.

Where to read

Select a good chair with a good light, a relaxed atmosphere, or use a desk or table, making yourself as comfortable as possible.

In noisy places, cultivate your powers of concentration so that you may learn without being distracted. Of course, do not become a non-communicating and withdrawn bore with family and friends.

How to read

Read consistently, consecutively, daily, dedicatedly and with enjoyment. Always keep a ball-point pen handy. Make notes. Underline passages. Mark your Bible.

Schedule a special period for reading, probably 20 minutes as a rock bottom period. Thirty minutes of Bible reading a day will do wonders for your spiritual life. Try early morning or an evening time.

Read for personal development with the definite purpose of making the Bible a practical guide for life. Read as though God were speaking directly to you. Perhaps He is.

Read expectantly and thoughtfully, asking, "What is God's message for me today? What does this passage teach me to believe?—to become?—to do? The more you are willing to listen, the more He will say.

Read with imagination, unhurriedly. Try to picture the scene and think of the characters as living people.

Use commentaries or expositions on each book of the Bible. In time, you can acquire your own study library for further study.

Do not be disturbed if there are some passages you do not understand.

Dig for hidden treasure by repeated readings.

Keep a record of what you have read.

Turn to the Bible each day, regardless of how you feel.

Bible reading plans

- Read through the Bible in a year, consecutively. Read four chapters a day, which you can easily do in about half an hour, if you do not get bogged down in theological questions prematurely, or pause to study instead of just reading.

There are 1,189 chapters in the Bible. By reading three in the Old Testament and one in the New Testament each day, you can finish in under a year, even if you miss a day every now and then. Or, you can pick up a daily Bible-reading guide at your Christian bookstore.

- Read through the Bible twice a year, about 7 chapters a day. Jim followed that plan at the age of 14.

- Follow a Bible reading plan like that set forth in *Search the Scriptures* (by G. T. Manley, Inter-Varsity Press) and spend your time going through the Bible in depth.

- Read a book at a sitting, like you would a short story or a novel, maybe on a Saturday or Sunday afternoon.

- Read a book a week if you are really serious about knowing the Word and want to learn it. Get *What the Bible is All About* by Henrietta Mears, and follow the 52-lesson reading and study program outlined in it.

- Read rapidly to get the gist and movement of the book, even if you do not comprehend all the details.

- Browse around through the Bible. It is a library. You see a title that interests you? Thumb through the pages of that particular book. Read the story of Joseph, or Moses, or the little love story of Ruth. Familiarize yourself with all the Bible's contents.

- We recommend that young people, especially, read the book of Proverbs every month for a year. With 31 chapters, it is a natural. This practical compendium of wisdom and psychology will add character and success to life.

- No Christian ought to read less than one chapter a day under any conditions.

- With the New Testament on tape or CD, you can listen while in the car or anywhere with a portable player. Listening is the very next thing to reading.

You may find and develop a better plan than any here suggested.

The important thing is to read, even if you only use a hop, skip and jump method. Something is always better than nothing.

But you will be wise to read systematically, thoughtfully, prayerfully, steadily, daily, moving through the entire Bible in a specified length of time, whether it be a few months, a year or longer.

Then when you have read it all and can recall the flow of biblical revelation, you will better be prepared to study in detail and in depth.

I have been reading and studying the Word of God for over 60 years now. Still His mercies are new every morning.

His mercies are still new every morning.

His word abides forever.

It is superpowerful and supernatural.

Read it!

Example to Follow

Robert L. Sumner, an evangelist, began reading ten chapters a day in 1940, finishing the Bible in four months. Following this plan, he read through three times in a year. In 2010, he completed his 210th read through the Bible.

19

How to Memorize the Scriptures

Thy word have I hid in mine heart, that I might not sin against thee (Psalm 119:11).

Committing verses and passages from the Word of God to memory is the most powerful method of Bible study discussed in this entire series. Saturating the heart and mind with biblical truth provides an underlying strength, a firm spiritual foundation, a reservoir of information readily available and the truth needed to share the gospel with another on the spur of the moment.

Every serious Christian who wants to please God should make every effort to memorize vital portions of the Bible.

Some people can easily read and remember. Memorization comes naturally. A few rare individuals have "photographic minds," recalling a page or a paragraph so vividly that they can be read by rote from the clear mental image in their minds.

Others simply erroneously imagine that they cannot memorize at all.

The truth is, most of us can memorize rather well if we only will invest time, concentration and deep interest in it.

Actors, particularly Shakespearian thespians, memorize thousands of lines, sometimes whole plays, in their pursuit of dramatic excellence.

How much more the dedicated believer needs to commit the Word to memory.

With thoughtful memorization comes deeper spirituality as the supernatural Word of God percolates through the mind, influencing decisions, thought patterns, plans, and most of all, the character.

You may select a planned memorization program

J. O. Grooms' *Treasure Path to Successful Soul Winning* is one of the finest systems ever devised. This dynamic personal soulwinner, who has seen tens of thousands of people profess Christ and who has taught multiplied thousands to memorize Scriptures and to win souls, is now the author of five small books, complete with Scriptures to memorize, fully printed out and in a logical sequence for the soulwinner's use.

Write to J.O. Grooms, Treasure Path to Soul Winning, Box 2104, Lynchburg, Virginia 24501, for full information.

Another widely-used program published by the Bible Memory Association is available. This also consists of pocket-sized booklets which can be carried anywhere. Such facility makes possible the utilization of spare moments for memorizing.

This author began memorizing verses on small 2 1/2" cards, produced by the "Navigators," an organization founded during World War II to reach servicemen. Using these cards, which could be carried in a shirt pocket, I committed to memory several hundred verses, which I still quote 40 years later, constituting the core of useful passages on the most important biblical subjects.

A fourth system, similar to the "Navigators" program since it is on small cards, is available at Christian bookstores. A small box of 175 cards imprinted with one or two verses can be procured and utilized.

You may originate your own plan

Take an old Bible, read through it, selecting verses you wish to memorize. Carefully cut out the verses and paste them on 3 x 5 cards, making any notes on the back of the cards you desire. Start with a set of 50 verses from the New Testament. Later, add another 50 selected verses.

You may prefer to memorize whole chapters at a time, making use of a *Scofield Reference Bible*, because every copy always has the same verse on the same place on the same page. Having read a Scofield Bible nearly every day for 42 years, I can quickly find most any passage by visualizing the page in my mind.

Plan your memorization program

One preacher I knew spent about an hour a day memorizing a chapter. It took him five years to memorize the New Testament, since he mastered one chapter a week. It revolutionized his whole ministry.

It is said that the great Bible teacher William Evans, who was a giant for God in the first half of the 20th century, could quote the entire Bible in English, the Old Testament in Hebrew, and the New Testament in Greek. He spent four hours a day reviewing or reading from memory.

Most of us will never attain such heights, but we can all memorize hundreds, perhaps thousands of verses, if we set our minds and hearts to the task.

Plan to do it. Get started. The sooner, the better!

Use various techniques

Take the verse or card with the verse on it and read it 10 times, once out loud. Turn the card away and try to repeat it. Continue reading and repeating, preferably out loud, until you can quote it verbatim. Give the reference before and after quoting the verse. There is no substitute for repetition. Concentration is vital. Think as you quote, and let the meaning sink into your soul. Try memorizing one verse a day. Then review, review, review. If you have a set of verses, review 10 or 20 verses a day, reading from memory, before you tackle a new verse.

With thoughtful memorization comes deeper spirituality as the supernatural Word of God percolates through the mind, influencing decisions, thought patterns, plans, and most of all, the character.

Set aside times for review, and use spare moments while waiting for a bus, sitting in an office, driving your car, or just anyplace. You can always use any spare moments at any time or place to review verses you have memorized. Make it part of your everyday life.

You may want to memorize a chapter or a book. Start with easy and famous chapters, like 1 Corinthians 13, translating the word "charity" as "love," since that is the primary meaning of the Greek word *agape*.

Go on to Hebrews 11, Romans 8, John 3, Ephesians 2, Colossians 1, or any chapter that you especially need in your life.

First, read the chapter over rapidly 10 or 15 times. Then read it out loud as many times as possible, say 5 or 10 times, thus familiarizing yourself with the content, terminology, wording, subjects and thrust of the chapter.

Then, concentrate on the first verse, using the same repetitive techniques previously discussed. Master the first verse, then the second. If you master a verse a day, you can actually average memorizing one chapter a month.

Now, there are those with special ability in memorization who can master the whole chapter by concentrated readings, the entire chapter being recorded in the mind as a speaker would memorize a speech. If that is your style, use it.

Do what works best for you.

The three "R's" of memorization

Read the verse or the passage over and over again. Keep reading it. Don't worry about all the subtle meanings at this time.

Review is an absolute necessity. Spend 10-20 minutes a day reviewing, or even up to an hour if you are serious about really memorizing the Word of God. Review will mean retention.

Relate or quote the verse to someone else. Relate it to your own life.

Use the verses in your Bible teaching, witnessing and preaching.

Out of over 31,000 verses in the Bible, your authors have memorized over 3,000 verses, or 10% of the Bible. You can memorize at least a few dozen verses.

We pray that someone who reads these words will resolve to memorize the whole New Testament in the next few years.

If any man lack wisdom, let him ask of God that giveth to all men liberally . . . (James 1:5).

20

HOW TO MARK YOUR BIBLE

Write it down. Always have a pen handy, and jot down thoughts, ideas, outlines, and points to ponder in a Bible study notebook. Use a lined spiral notebook or a loose-leaf notebook, or devise your own system with which you are comfortable. But make it a conscious, constant habit to write out your thoughts in outline form, at least as you read and study the Word.

But also mark your Bible. Making notations, drawing lines, or using your own method of emphasis will greatly enhance your knowledge of the Bible. Never imagine that there is something especially sanctified about the pages of the Bible that would prohibit you from writing all over the margin or between lines.

Methods of marking

- There are on the market color-coded Bibles. A few special subjects like salvation, the second coming, or Christian living are not only indicated by notes, but also by superimposed color over the Scripture on the subject. This is useful for newer Christians who are unfamiliar with where basic subjects are covered. More mature students may find the heavy color more of a nuisance than a help.

- Some Bibles already have underlining either in black or in some color (different colors for different subjects), also most helpful to newer Christians.

- Most growing Bible students will want to mark their own Bibles, underling passages that seem especially relevant or useful. Some prefer colored pens or highlighters and devise their own color coding, using red, for instance, for salvation, blue for the second coming, yellow for Christian living, purple for heaven, others just use black for everything.

A time-honored system

"The Underlines and Railways method."

The horizontal lines under words are called "underlines." The diagonal lines connecting words or ideas can be called "railways."

In any given verse, underline only the word or words required to convey the thought; leaving other words to be underlined in connection with other thoughts which may occur hereafter.

It often occurs that "railways" are connected with two or three separate parts of one verse. This can only be expressed by carefully observing the above rule.

Draw the lines with a small thin ruler. Railways should be made at the same angle, thus interfering less with the wording on the page.

If a "railway" is connecting an idea or word that appears again on the next page, draw it at the margin's edge and write the reference.

Freely write in your own references to other passages.

Try to print plainly and legibly with a fine-point pen.

What to look for

Look for similar words or expressions. In Matthew 8 and 9, look for the word "behold." Connect its uses with "railways."

Watch for comparisons and contrasts. Count the number of items in a list (Galatians 5:22; 1 Corinthians 6:9,10). Look for repetition of phrases, such as "Know ye not?" in the books of 1 Corinthians and Romans . . . or the word "immediately" in the Gospel of Mark . . . the word "overcome" in the Book of Revelation, chapters 2 and 3.

21

HOW TO SEARCH SCRIPTURES ON THE INTERNET

Logos Bible Software has a great host of tools to help you see the trees. Lexical tags in the various tagged editions of the GNT (including the various interlinears and reverse interlinears) link to lexicons and help you find the range of meanings possible for a given word. Morphological tags in the same texts provide some contextual clues to help determine the meaning and use of the word in the particular instance under study. Learning grammars help students recognize the most common morphological and lexical trees for themselves.

But, while one can learn a lot of useful things by examining the trees, some of the greatest riches of studying the New Testament in Greek come when you can step back and see the forest. That is, at some point the student needs to look at things above the word level. 'Syntax' is the term we use for describing how words form into phrases and clauses, and how those structures are used to form sentences. Logos Bible Software has tools for working at the syntax level as well. Reference grammars tend to contain a lot of word- (tree-) level detail on areas like morphology (how words are formed) and phonology (how a language sounds), but they will frequently contain some good information on larger structures like phrases and clauses as well. But few reference grammars approach the Greek New Testament above the level of the sentence. In 2008 Logos Bible Software released an edition of the OpenText.org syntax database, which graphs out sentence, clause and phrase relationships and provides a powerful searching interface for working at the syntactic level. Other syntax databases for the Greek New Testament are also in the works.

There are, however, a growing number of scholars who are looking at much larger units of text than the sentence. The branch of linguistics dedicated to looking at larger blocks of text and analyzing how language is used to convey meaning on a much broader scale is 'discourse analysis'. ('Text-linguistics' is another term sometimes applied to this field.) Recent posts on this blog by Dr. Runge have been giving you a taste of some of the data we've been working on to show discourse level features. But I wanted to call your attention to a new collection of books just posted on the prepub page. The Studies in New Testament Greek Collection contains a number of insightful books and essays on the topic of discourse analysis. The books provide some of the theories for how to analyze texts, and then apply the theories so you can see the results. This collection introduces other fields related to discourse analysis, such as 'rhetorical criticism' (an examination of how authors use various language elements to persuade or make an argument) and essays on how the cultural context of the New Testament should inform our exegesis. (For example, there are many essays on the topic of how bilingualism in 1st Century Palestine should effect how we read the New Testament.)

If you skim the authors and editors of the volumes in this set, you'll notice several by Stanley Porter (Author of Idioms of the Greek New Testament) and Jeffrey T. Reed (with Stanley Porter, one of the OpenText.org fellows) as well as D.A. Carson (author of *Exegetical Fallacies*), just to name a few. In addition to discourse and rhetoric, there are many essays in this collection that treat on other intersections between linguistics and biblical studies. This collection serves as an excellent introduction to the value of linguistics for interpreters of scripture.

Other internet resources

If you have internet access, there are excellent web sites that provide helpful tools for Bible study.

www.BibleGateway.com

www.soniclight.com/constable/notes.htm.

This is the web site of Dr. Thomas Constable, professor of Bible Exposition at Dallas Theological Seminary. He has put together, for public use, excellent notes on every book of the Bible.

22

How to Practice What You Learn

Who has not heard the old adage, "Practice what you preach" spoken many times? Failure to respond to clear-cut, plain teachings from the Word of God not only dims our testimony, but robs us of personal blessings.

Head knowledge must be coupled with heart knowledge, lest we be hearers and not doers of the Word.

> *But be ye doers of the word, and not hearers only, deceiving your own selves. For if any be a hearer of the word and not a doer, he is like unto a man beholding his natural face in a glass: For he beholdeth himself, and goeth his way, and straightway forgetteth what manner of man he was. But whoso looketh into the perfect law of liberty, and continueth therein, he being not a forgetful hearer, but a doer of the work, this man shall be blessed in his deed* (James 1:22-25).

Take Bible truth *personally*
As you read the New Testament, especially, jot down specific commands and instructions that are applicable to your own personal life. Endeavor each day to focus on some biblical exhortation, resolving to respond obediently. All of the epistles are full of helpful spiritual admonitions, principles and practices requiring diligent attention.

Apply teaching to yourself first!
Remember that everyone must "give an account of himself [herself] to God."

Avoid judgmentalism.
It is so easy to see the beam in someone else's eye and miss the mote in one's

own; to be ready to apply a passage to another only.

In the Sermon on the Mount, Jesus dealt severely with this self-right-eous, self-justifying approach, saying,

> *Thou hypocrite, first cast out the beam out of thine own eye, and then shalt thou see clearly to cast out the mote out of thy brother's eye* (Matthew 7:5).

All too often, judgmentalism of others is a form of self-praise—psychologically, and perhaps subconsciously, trying to feel better about ourselves by putting down someone else, imagining that we are better than they because we do not fall short in the same way they do.

Affirm your own commitment.
Spirituality must be constantly renewed. Yesterday's manna may grow stale today. Each day, affirm your personal desire to please God.

> *If any man will come after me, let him take up his cross daily and follow me* (Luke 9:23).

Seek Bible wisdom *prayerfully*
Ask for wisdom from the Word before you read and study.

> *If any man lack wisdom, let him ask of God, that giveth to all men liberally and upbraideth not, and it shall be given him* (James 1:5).

Associate with godly believers
Seek out as your best friends those who share your spiritual values. While we want to have friends who are not yet in the fold in order that we might eventually win them, you will want to cultivate warm, spiritual friendships with brothers and sisters in Christ.

Attend church and Sunday School regularly, and listen to your pastor teach and preach.
Since he is the shepherd of the flock, he is your leader and guide. His teaching takes precedence over the divergent and varying views of different radio and television preachers you might hear. If you have serious questions, ask

him for the answers from the Word. Prayerfully listen and take notes as he breaks the bread of life.

Absorb the Bible's truth *powerfully*

Since the Holy Spirit is the author, He knows what it means, and He desires to enable you to make it real in your life.

> *Howbeit when he, the Spirit of truth, is come, he will guide you into all truth; for he shall not speak of himself; but whatsoever he shall hear, that shall he speak: and he will show you things to come* (John 16:13).

While this passage deals with the divine inspiration of the New Testament books primarily, the Spirit is with you to illuminate the Word and to impart power for you to put in practice the things you learn.

Bear in mind that the Old Testament Law was primarily for Israel and for the Dispensation of Law; therefore, the detailed dietary and cultural rules for that day are supplanted by the clear teachings of Christ and of His apostles in this Dispensation of Grace. "We are not under law, but under grace."

Yield your life, your mind, and your heart to the Holy Spirit.
Thereby you will be in the proper spiritual frame of mind to be obedient.

Confess your sins and faults to the Lord.

> *If we confess our sins, he is faithful and just to forgive us our sins and to cleanse us from all unrighteousness* (1 John 1:9).

Unconfessed sins will clog the flow of spiritual blessings into our lives and prevent us from applying Bible truths to our hearts.

Follow Christ *purposefully*

Christ's indwelling presence, lived through us, is the essence of genuine Christianity in this life. Our compliance with the Word of God is the external counterpart of His internal operation with our souls. We will never be totally like Him until we see Him as He is, but the constant lifelong process of ever becoming more like him is the practice of spirituality.

For to me to live is Christ, and to die is gain (Philippians 1:21).

Bettering your life and testimony is growth in grace.
Believing God always, as the Word encourages, is walking by faith, for "the just shall live by faith."

Emphasize what God stresses *particularly*

Matters which God emphasizes most in His Word, both in the number of passages dealing with a subject and in the obvious importance the Lord attaches to it, should receive greater attention.

Majoring on the majors of prayer, faith, love, the Holy Spirit, biblical doctrines, godliness, and all the principles that vitally affect our lives and testimonies is always the course of wisdom.

Overstressing peripheral cultural practices, supposing that Christianity is mainly external and not primarily internal, leads to majoring on the minors.

Keep studying and growing *permanently*

Never falsely suppose you know all about the Bible and need no further instruction. Remember always that "His mercies are new every morning."

Resist the temptation to coast in your Christian life, for our pilgrimage is upwards toward "the city which hath foundations whose builder and maker is God." You can only coast a short distance before the downward pull of the world will result in your spiritual decline.

By staying close to the Master Teacher and meditating in His Word every day, always seeking to follow Christ and obey His commands, you will be "practicing what you preach."

I charge you by the Lord that this epistle be read unto all the holy brethren (1 Thessalonians 5:27).

22

How to Preach and Teach What You Learn

And the things that thou hast heard of me among many witnesses, the same commit thou to faithful men, who shall be able to teach others, also (2 Timothy 2:2).

After all, studying and learning the Word for one's self is to gain great personal life enrichment, but no one should desire merely to hoard the truth, not spreading the gospel and the Word of God to others.

The more we learn, the more we have to give to others.

Through these lessons, we have explored 16 ways to approach the Word in studying. A number of helpful tools, useful for reference and research, have been suggested. Vital hermeneutical principles for understanding the Bible have been presented. Constantly, gentle reader, you have been urged to get into the Word of God until the Word of God gets into you.

Now, in conclusion, this writer challenges you to spread the gospel, teach and preach the Word, and share the message of the Lord with others at every opportunity.

Witnessing to the lost

D. L. Moody used to make a personal presentation of the gospel to one individual every day, seeking God's leadership as to the person to whom he should speak. You might not come into contact with that many people, and will want to make a special project of talking to one person for sure each week. Every Christian, even a homebody, can do that.

Others have written well on soulwinning. Get some materials that you can use.

Learn how to use the ROMANS ROAD, popularized by the dynamic Jack Hyles of the First Baptist Church of Hammond, Indiana. Start with Romans 3:10-12; move on to 3:23; turn to 6:23; pause with Romans 5:12; then move on to Romans 10:9,10,13. Underline the verses and be able to quote or read them.

Others prefer the JOURNEY THROUGH JOHN, emphasizing the new birth. Start with John 3:3 and 5. Move on to chapter 5:24; turn back to 3:18 and 36; stress the death of Christ from 10:9-11; touch on 10:27-29 to show how you can be saved and know it. Come back to John 1:12 for a

Spread the gospel, teach and preach the Word, share the message of the Lord with others at every opportunity.

close. Use these verses as suggestions and build from them your presentation of the gospel.

Another excellent way to present the Gospel is to acquire the colorful 16-page booklet entitled *Jesus Saves,* prepared by Lee Fredrickson.

Remember, you do not have to quote a thousand verses to win souls. Just use one of these simple methods with an open Bible, telling, also how Jesus saved you.

Sharing with other believers

If you find some special spiritual truth or devotional thought each day in the Word, share it with someone else who knows Christ. It can be your husband, your wife, your friend, a Christian coworker.

Dr. Walter L. Wilson used to ask all Christians he met, "Do you have some wonderful truth out of the Word for today that you can share with me?"

Avoid being argumentative or sarcastic in any way as you talk to other Christian friends about the Word. You want to be a blessing, not a hindrance. You want to help edify one another as the Lord so encourages.

Teaching a Bible class

As a Sunday School teacher, you will want to equip your pupils with truths that will help them be victorious Christians.

How to prepare the lesson

- Read over the passage you are going to teach several times. Then focus on the dominant idea or truth you want to stress. That is your underlying theme for the lesson.

- Originate a title for your lesson which may be a catch phrase to which you will refer in the lesson, or it may suggest the content of the passage. The more unique the title, without being bizarre, the better. This will stimulate interest.

- Prepare an outline for the lesson, always strongly emphasizing the Scriptures themselves.

- Prayerfully write out an interesting introduction geared to arouse interest and spark thinking in your pupils' minds.

- Think through your conclusion in which you will apply the truths presented, and call for some action or decision based on the lesson. Write this out.

- Use any and all of the techniques discussed in this series to enhance your personal study.

- Pray for spiritual illumination before, during and after your period of preparation.

How to present the lesson.
Notice these "R's."

- *Read* the passage or a portion of it very distinctly at the start of the teaching session. Then pause for public prayer.

- *Restate* your title and explain the theme of the lesson.

- *Repeat* in advance some of your main points for emphasis.

- *Relate* each section or point to the needs of the people there. Try to have a short illustration for each point.

- *Review* the main ideas you want to implant in the hearts of your hearers as you close.

- *Remember* to conclude in prayer and call for commitment, change or application of the truth presented.

Ye ought to be teachers . . . (Hebrews 5:12).

Preaching the Word

Teaching may be defined as expressing the truth; preaching is seeking to get people to accept the truth.

While much can be said about preaching styles, homiletical research and the communication of truth, let me summarize it in these few points.

- Pray before you study, as you study, as you get up to preach, and after you preach. Spiritual, prevailing prayer will bring something to preaching that nothing else can . . . the flow of the power of God.

- Prepare every message well. Use all the approaches to Bible study we have suggested at one time or another. Make copious notes. Give attention to your opening and your close. Absorb into your heart and soul the passage of Scripture or the text you are going to expound.

- Preach the Word with vigor, interest, heart, simplicity, depth, enthusiasm, courage, and most of all, the power of God. Emphasize! Illustrate! Reiterate! Do not be a slave to your notes, unless your style is reading the manuscript which can be done very well if you really learn how.

- Plead with sinners. Our supreme purpose is to communicate the gospel. Give the plan of salvation in practically every message.

Well, if you have journeyed with us through all of these 22 lessons, we are glad to have had your company. We trust you will be the better for it.

We desire only God's best for you. We close by repeating the prayer of the Psalmist in 119:18:

Open thou mine eyes that I may behold wondrous things out of thy law.

A Challenge

Search the Scriptures Daily

The challenge that comes to people today, busy as they are in various projects, is to allocate periods of time for pursuing the wisdom of God in Sacred Scripture.

"Study to show thyself approved unto God, a workman that needeth not to be ashamed, rightly dividing the Word of Truth (2 Timothy 2:15).

Delving deep into the mysteries of God, as variously set forth in the divinely-inspired Word of God, must be the prime practice of the called preacher and teacher of the Holy Gospel in our times. Saturate your mind, immerse your thoughts into Sacred Scripture, thus bringing every thought into captivity unto the obedience of Christ.

We must live, if we are to please God, in accordance with His will, as totally dedicated men and women, whose delight is in the Law of the Lord. In this law and His promises we must meditate day and night.

Then we will make our way prosperous and then we will have good success.

The following pages are selected from:
365 Ways to Know God

God Wants You to Know Him on a First-Name Basis

by Elmer L. Towns

The Bible has more than 1,000 names, titles and metaphors for God: El Shaddai, Shepherd, King, Father, Son and Prophet are only a few of them. Each name and title of God represents one aspect of Who He is. As a person, you are known by your given name in addition to titles, such as parent, spouse and friend. The more you are and do, the more names and titles you have. God, the creator of the universe and every living creature therein, has facets to His nature that extend beyond our imaginings, and countless names to describe each of His attributes.

In *365 Ways to Know God*, you will reflect on one name of God for every day of the year, nurturing a deep, worshipful understanding of Him so that you can come to know Him on a first-name basis. Your daily devotionals are a dialogue between you and God. You will begin by prayerfully expressing a need, and then read on as God unveils the meaning of one of His many names and how He can use it to remove your daily burdens.

This is a guide for the heart, demonstrating God's ability and willingness to answer your every hope and need from the boundless reservoirs of His love.

Used by permission from the author.

Appendix 1: The Names of the Lord (Jehovah) in the Old Testament

Adonai Jehovah – The Lord God (Genesis 15:2)

Hamelech Jehovah – The LORD, the King (Psalm 98:6)

Jehovah – The LORD (Exodus 6:2-3)

Jehovah Adon Kol Ha'arets – The LORD, the Lord of All the Earth (Joshua 3:13)

Jehovah Bore – The LORD Creator (Isaiah 40:28)

Jehovah Eli – The LORD My God (Psalm 18:2)

Jehovah 'Elyon – The LORD Most High (Psalm 7:17)

Jehovah Gibbor Milchamah – The LORD Mighty in Battle (Psalm 24:8)

Jehovah Go'el – The LORD Thy Redeemer (Isaiah 49:26; 60:16)

Jehovah Hashopet – The LORD the Judge (Judges 11:27)

Jehovah Hoshe'ah – The LORD Save (Psalm 20:9)

Jehovah 'Immekha – The LORD Is with You (Judges 6:12)

Jehovah 'Izuz We Gibbor – The LORD Strong and Mighty (Psalm 24:8)

Jehovah Jireh – The LORD Will Provide (Genesis 22:14)

Jehovah Kabodhi – The LORD My Glory (Psalm 3:3)

Jehovah Keren-Yish'i – The LORD the Horn of My Salvation (Psalm 18:2)

Jehovah Khereb – The LORD . . . the Sword (Deuteronomy 33:29)

Jehovah Machsi – The LORD My Refuge (Psalm 91:9)

Jehovah Magen – The LORD, the Shield (Deuteronomy 33:29)

Jehovah Maginnenu – The LORD Our Defence (Psalm 89:18)

Jehovah Makheh – The LORD That Smiteth (Ezekiel 7:9)

Jehovah Ma'oz – The LORD ... My Fortress (Jeremiah 16:19)

Jehovah Ma'oz Khayyay – The LORD the Strength of My Life (Psalm 27:1)

Jehovah Melek 'Olam – The LORD King Forever (Psalm 10:16; Isaiah 6:5)

Jehovah Mephalti – The LORD My Deliverer (Psalm 18:2)

Jehovah Meqaddishkhem – The LORD Our Sanctifier (Exodus 31:13)

Jehovah Metsudhathi – The LORD . . . My Fortress (Psalm 18:2)

Jehovah Misgabbi – The LORD My High Tower (Psalm 18:2)

Jehovah Moshi'ekh – The LORD Thy Savior (Isaiah 49:26; 60:16)

Jehovah Nissi – The LORD Our Banner (Exodus 17:15)

Jehovah 'Ori – The LORD My Light (Psalm 27:1)

Jehovah "Oz-Lamo – The LORD the Strength of His people (Psalm 28:7)

Jehovah Qanna – The LORD, Whose Name Is Jealous (Exodus 34:14)

Jehovah Ro'i – The LORD My Shepherd (Psalm 23:1)

Jehovah Rophe – The LORD That Healeth (Exodus 15:26)

Jehovah Sabaoth – The LORD of Hosts (1 Samuel 1:3)

Jehovah Sal'i – The LORD My Rock (Psalm 18:2)

Jehovah Shalom – The LORD Our Peace (Judges 6:24)

Jehovah Shammah – The LORD Is There (Ezekiel 48:35)

Jehovah Tsidqenu – The LORD Our Righteousness (Jeremiah 23:6)

Jehovah Tsuri – O LORD, My Strength (Psalm 19:14)

Jehovah 'Uzam – The LORD Their Strength (Psalm 37:39)

Appendix 2: The Names of the Lord God (Jehovah Elohim; Kurios Ho Theos) in Scripture

Holy LORD God
(1 Samuel 6:20)

LORD God
(*Jehovah Elohim*; Genesis 2:4)

LORD God . . . Abounding in
Goodness (Exodus 34:6)

LORD God . . . Abounding in
Truth (Exodus 34:6)

Lord God Almighty (Revelation
4:8)

LORD God . . . Gracious
(Exodus 34:6)

LORD God, Judge of All the
Earth (Genesis 18:25)

LORD God . . . Long-suffering
(Exodus 34:6)

LORD God Merciful
(Exodus 34:6)

LORD, God Most High
(*Jehovah El Elyon*; Genesis
14:22; Psalm 18:13)

LORD God of Abraham, Isaac,
and Israel (1 Kings 18:36)

LORD God of Elijah
(2 Kings 2:14)

LORD God of Gods (*El
Elohim Jehovah*; Joshua 22:22)

LORD God of Heaven
(Genesis 24:7)

LORD God of Hosts (*Jehovah
Elohim Tseba'oth*; 2 Samuel 5:10)

LORD God of the Hebrews
(Exodus 3:18)

Lord God of the Holy Prophets
(Revelation 22:6)

LORD God of Israel (*Jehovah
Elohe Yisra'el*; Exodus 5:1)

LORD God of My Lord the
King (1Kings 1:36)

LORD God of My Master
Abraham
(Genesis 24:12, 27, 42, 48)

LORD, God of My Salvation
(*Jehovah Elohe Yeshu'athi*; Psalm
88:1)

LORD God of Truth
(*Jehovah El 'Emeth*; Psalm 31:5)

LORD God of Your Fathers
(*Jehovah Elohe 'Abothekhem*;
Exodus 3:15)

LORD God Omnipotent
(Revelation 19:6)

LORD God Who Judges Her
(Revelation 18:8)

LORD Is a God of Justice
(Isaiah 30:18)

LORD Is God of the Hills
(1 Kings 20:28)

LORD Is God of the Valleys
(see 1 Kings 20:28)

LORD Is My Helper
(Hebrews 13:6; Psalm 32:7)

LORD Is My Strength and
Song (Exodus 15:2)

LORD Is the God of
Knowledge (1 Samuel 2:3)

LORD Is the God of
Recompense (*Jehovah El
Gemuloth;* Jeremiah 51:56)

LORD Is the Great God
(Psalm 95:3)

LORD, Mighty in Battle
(Psalm 24:8)

LORD, Pillar of Fire
(Exodus 13:21-22)

LORD, the Everlasting God
(*Jehovah El Olam;* Genesis
21:33)

LORD, the God of All Flesh
(Jeremiah 32:27)

LORD, the God of David Your
Father (2 Kings 20:5)

LORD, the God of Heaven and
the God of Earth
(Genesis 24:3)

LORD, the God of Shem
(Genesis 9:26)

LORD, the God of the Spirits
of All Flesh (Numbers 27:16)

LORD, the Window Opener
(see Malachi 3:10)

LORD, Thy Exceedingly Great
Reward (Genesis 15:1)

Appendix 3: The Names of God (Elohim) in Scripture

Almighty God
(*El Shaddai*; Genesis 17:1)

Eternal God
(Deuteronomy 33:27)

Everlasting God (Isaiah 40:28)

Faithful God
(*El Emunah*; Deuteronomy 7:9)

Father to Those Who Have No Father (Psalm 68:5)

God (*Elohim*; Genesis 1:1)

God Almighty (Genesis 28:3)

God in Heaven (*Elohim Bashamayim*; Joshua 2:11)

God Is a Refuge for Us (*Elohim Machaseh Lanu*; Psalm 62:8)

God Is My Helper
(*Elohim 'Ozer Li*; Psalm 54:4)

God Most High
(*El 'Elyon*; Genesis 14:18)

God Most High
(*Elohim "Elyon*; Psalm 57:2)

God My Exceeding Joy
(*El Simchath Gili*; Psalm 43:4)

God, My King
(*Eli Malki*; Psalm 68:24)

God My Rock
(*El Sela'*; Psalm 42:9)

God of Abraham
(Genesis 31:42)

God of All Comfort
(2 Corinthians 1:3)

God of All Grace (1 Peter 5:10)

God of All the Families of Israel (Jeremiah 31:1)

God of Bethel (Genesis 31:13)

God of Daniel (Daniel 6:26)

God of Forgiveness (*Elohim Selichot*; Nehemiah 9:17)

God of Glory
(*El Hakabodh*; Psalm 29:3)

God of Gods
(Deuteronomy 10:17)

God of Heaven (Ezra 5:12)

God of Heaven and Earth
(Ezra 5:11)

God of His Father David
(2 Chronicles 34:3)

God of Hope (Romans 15:13)

God of Hosts
(*Elohim Tsaba'oth;* Psalm 80:7)
God of Isaac (Genesis 28:13)

God of Israel
(*Elope Yisra'el;* Exodus 24:10)

God of Jacob
(*Elope Ya'akob;* 2 Samuel 23:1)

God of Jerusalem
(2 Chronicles 32:19)

God of Jeshurun (Deuteronomy
33:26)

God of Judgment
(Malachi 2:17)

God of Love
(2 Corinthians 13:11)

God of My Father
(Genesis 31:5)

God of My Life
(*El Khayyay;* Psalm 42:8)

God of My Praise
(Psalm 109:1)

God of My Righteousness
(*Elohe Tsidqi;* Psalm 4:1)

God of My Salvation
(*Elohe Yish'i;* Psalm 18:46)

God of My Strength
(*Elohe Ma'uzi;* Psalm 43:2)

God of Nahor (Genesis 31:53)
God of Our Lord Jesus Christ
(Ephesians 1:17)

God of Patience (Romans 15:5)

God of Peace (Romans 15:33)

God of Shadrach, Meshach and
Abednego (Daniel 3:29)

God of the Armies of Israel
(1 Samuel 17:45)

God of the Beginning
(see Deuteronomy 33:27)

God of the Earth
(Revelation 11:4)

God of the Gentiles
(Romans 3:29)

God of the Hebrews
(Exodus 5:3)

God of the House of God
(*El Bethel;* Genesis 35:7)

God of the Jews (Romans 3:29)

God of the Land
(2 Kings 17:26)

God of the Living
(see Matthew 22:32)

God of Truth
(Deuteronomy 32:4)

God of Your Father Abraham
(Genesis 26:24)
God, the God of Israel
(*El Elohe Israel;* Genesis 33:20)

God Who Avenges Me
(*El Nekamoth;* Psalm 18:47)

God Who Forgives
(*El Nose';* Psalm 99:8)

God Who Is Near
(Jeremiah 23:23-24)

God Who Judges the Earth
(*Elohim Shophtim Ba'arets;* Psalm 58:11)

God Who Sees Me
(*El Roi;* Genesis 16:13)

Great God
(Deuteronomy 10:17)
Holy God
(*Elohim Qedoshim;* Joshua 24:19)

Jealous God
(*El Qanna;* Exodus 20:5)

Living God
(*El Khay;* Joshua 3:10)

Merciful God
(*Elohe Khasdi;* Psalm 59:10)

Mighty God
(*El Gibbor;* Jeremiah 32:18)

Unknown God (Acts 17:23)

Voice (Psalm 18:13)

Appendix 4: Preeminent Pronouns of The Father in Scripture

Abba Father (Mark 14:36)

Ancient of Days (Daniel 7:13)

Creator of the Ends of the Earth (Isaiah 40:28)

Father (1 John 3:1)

Father and the Son (1 John 2:22)

Father in Spirit (John 4:23)

Father, Lord of Heaven and Earth (Matthew 11:25)

Father of Glory (Ephesians 1:17)

Father of Lights (James 1:17)

Father of Mercies (2 Corinthians 1:3)

Father of Our Lord (Ephesians 3:14)

Father of Our Lord Jesus (Romans 15:6; 2 Corinthians 1:3; Colossians 1:3)

Father of Spirits (Hebrews 12:9)

Father of the Fatherless (Psalm 68:5)

Father Which Art in Heaven (Matthew 6:9)

God and Father (James 3:9, *NKJV*)

God and Our Father (Ephesians 1:2)

God, Even the Father (1 Corinthians 15:24)

God of My Fathers (Acts 24:14)

God Our Father (Romans 1:7)

God the Father (John 6:27)

Heavenly Father (Matthew 6:14)

His Name Is Father (John 5:43)

Holy Father (John 17:11)

Living Father (John 6:57)

My Father (Matthew 7:21; John 10:29-30)

My Father and Your Father (John 20:17)

My Father Is the Husbandman (John 15:1)

My Father Worketh (John 5:17)

One Father, Even God (John 8:41)

One God and Father (1 Corinthians 8:6)

Our Father in Heaven (Luke 11:2, *NKJV*)

Righteous Father (John 17:25)

Spiritual Father (Hebrews 12:9, *CEV*)

Very God of Peace (1 Thessalonians 5:23)

Witness of God (1 John 5:9)

Your Father in Heaven (Matthew 5:16,45,48)

Appendix 5: Names, Titles, Metaphors, Figures of Speech And Pictures of Jesus

Advocate with the Father
(1 John 2:1)

Alien unto My Mother's
Children (Psalm 69:8)

Alive for Evermore
(Revelation 1:18)

All and in All (Colossians 3:11)

Almighty Which Is
(Revelation 1:18)

Alpha and Omega
(Revelation1:18)

Altar (Hebrews 13:10)

Altogether Lovely
(Song of Solomon 5:16)

Amen (Revelation 3:14)

Angel of God (Genesis 21:17)

Angel of His Presence
(Isaiah 63:9)

Angel of the Covenant (Malachi
3:1)

Angel of the Lord
(Genesis 16:7)

Anointed of God
(1 Samuel 2:35; Psalm 2:2)

Another King (Acts 17:7)

Apostle of Our Profession
(Hebrews 3:1)

Ark of the Covenant
(Joshua 3:3)

Arm of the Lord (Isaiah 53:1)

Author of Eternal Salvation
(Hebrews 5:9)

Author of Our Faith
(Hebrews 12:2)

Babe of Bethlehem
(Luke 2:12,16)

Balm in Gilead (Jeremiah 8:22)

Banner to Them That Fear
Thee (Psalm 60:4)

Bearer of Glory
(Zechariah 6:13)

Bearer of Sin (Hebrews 9:28)

Beauties of Holiness
(Psalm 110:3)

Before All Things
(Colossians 1:17)

Beginning (Colossians 1:18)

Beginning and the Ending
(Revelation 1:8)

Beginning of the Creation of
God (Revelation 3:14)

Beloved (Ephesians 1:6)

Beloved Son (Matthew 3:17)

Better (Hebrews 7:7)

Bishop of Your Souls
(1 Peter 2:25)

Blessed and Only Potentate
(1 Timothy 6:15)

Blessed for Evermore
(2 Corinthians 11:31)

Blessed Hope (Titus 2:13)

Branch (Zechariah 3:8; 6:12)

Branch of the Lord (Isaiah 4:2)

Branch of Righteousness
(Jeremiah 33:15)

Branch out of His Roots (Isaiah
11:1)

Bread of God (John 6:33)

Bread of Life (John 6:35)

Breaker (Micah 2:13)

Bridegroom of the Bride
(John 3:29)

Bright and Morning Star
(Revelation 22:16)

Brightness of His Glory
(Hebrews 1:3)

Brightness of Thy Rising (Isaiah
60:3)

Brother (Matthew 12:50)

Buckler (Psalm 18:30)

Builder of the Temple
(Zechariah 6:12-13)

Bundle of Myrrh
(Song of Solomon 1:13)

Captain of the Hosts of the
Lord (Joshua 5:14-15)

Captain of Their Salvation
(Hebrews 2:10)

Carpenter's Son
(Matthew 13:55)

Certain Nobleman
(Luke 19:12)

Certain Samaritan
(Luke 10:33)

Chief Cornerstone
(Ephesians 2:20; 1 Peter 2:6)

Chief Shepherd (1 Peter 5:4)

Chiefest Among Ten Thousand
(Song of Solomon 5:10)

Child Born (Isaiah 9:6)

Child Jesus (Luke 2:27-43)

Child of the Holy Ghost
(Matthew 1:18)

Chosen of God
(Luke 23:35; 1 Peter 2:4)

Chosen out of the People
(Psalm 89:19)

Christ (Matthew 1:16)

Christ a King (Luke 23:2)

Christ Come in the Flesh
(1 John 4:2)

Christ Crucified
(1 Corinthians 1:23)

Christ Jesus (Acts 19:4)

Christ Jesus Our Lord
(2 Corinthian 4:5)

Christ of God (Luke 9:20)

Christ Our Passover
(1 Corinthians 5:7)

Christ Risen from the Dead
(1 Corinthians 15:20)

Christ the Lord (Luke 2:11)

Cleft of the Rock
(Exodus 33:22)

Cloud (1 Corinthians 10:1)

Cluster of Camphire
(Song of Solomon 1:14)

Column of Smoke
(see Exodus 13:21)

Comforter (John 14:16-18)

Commander of the Hosts of the
Lord (Joshua 5:14-15)

Commander to the People
(Isaiah 55:4)

Conceived of the Holy Spirit
(Matthew 1:20)

Consolation of Israel
(Luke 2:25)

Corn of Wheat (John 12:24)

Counselor (Isaiah 9:6)

Covenant of the People
(Isaiah 42:6; 49:8)

Covert from the Tempest
(Isaiah 32:2)

Covert of Thy Wings
(Psalm 61:4)

Creator (Romans 1:25)

Crown of Glory (Isaiah 28:5)

Darling (Psalm 22:20)

David (Matthew 1:17)

Day (2 Peter 1:19)

Daysman Between Us
(Job 9:33)

Dayspring from on High
(Luke 1:78)

Daystar (2 Peter 1:19)

Dear Son (Colossians 1:13)

Deceiver (Matthew 27:63)

Defense (Psalm 94:22)

Deliverance of Zion (Joel 2:32)

Deliverer (Psalm 40:17)

Desire of All Nations
(Haggai 2:7)

Despised by the People
(Psalm 22:6)

Dew of Israel (Hosea 14:5)

Diadem of Beauty (Isaiah 28:5)

Door (John 10:9)

Door of the Sheep (John 10:7)

Dwelling Place (Psalm 90:1)

Elect (Isaiah 42:1)

Eliakim (Isaiah 22:20)

Elijah (Matthew 16:14)

Emmanuel (Matthew 1:23)

End of the Law (Romans 10:4)

Ensign of the People
(Isaiah 11:10)

Equal with God
(Philippians 2:6)

Eternal God
(Deuteronomy 33:27)

Eternal Life (1 John 1:2)

Everlasting Father (Isaiah 9:6)

Everlasting Light (Isaiah 60:19-
20)

Everlasting Name
(Isaiah 63:12)

Excellency (Job 13:11)

Excellency of Our God
(Isaiah 35:2)

Excellent (Psalm 8:1,9)

Express Image of His Person
(Hebrews 1:3)

Face of the Lord (Luke 1:76)

Fairer than the Children of
Men (Psalm 45:2)

Faithful (1 Thessalonians 5:24)

Faithful and True
(Revelation 19:11)

Faithful and True Witness
(Revelation 3:14)

Faithful Creator (1 Peter 4:19)

Faithful High Priest
(Hebrews 2:17)

Faithful Priest (1 Samuel 2:35)

Faithful Witness
(Revelation 1:5)

Faithful Witness Between Us
(Jeremiah 42:5)

Faithful Witness in Heaven
(Psalm 89:37)

Father (Psalm 89:26)

Feast (1 Corinthians 5:8)

Fellow (Zechariah 13:7)

Finisher of the Faith
(Hebrews 12:2)

First and the Last
(Revelation 1:8)

First Begotten (Hebrews 1:6)

First Begotten of the Dead

(Revelation 1:5; "Firstborn from
the Dead," *NKJV*)

Firstborn (Hebrews 12:23)

Firstborn Among Many
Brethren (Romans 8:29)

Firstborn of Every Creature
(Colossians 1:15)

Firstborn Son (Luke 2:7)

Firstfruit (Romans 11:16)

Firstfruits of Them That Sleep
(1 Corinthians 15:20)

Flag (see Isaiah 11:10)

Flesh (John 1:14)

Foolishness of God (1
Corinthians 1:25)

Foreordained Before the
Foundation of the World
(1 Peter 1:20)

Forerunner (Hebrews 6:20)

Fortress (Psalm 18:2)

Foundation Which Is Laid
(1 Corinthians 3:11)

Fountain of Life (Psalm 36:9)

Fountain of Living Waters
(Jeremiah 17:13)

Free Gift (Romans 5:15)

Friend of Publicans and Sinners
(Matthew 11:9; Luke 7:34)

Friend That Sticketh Closer
than a Brother (Proverbs 18:24)

Fruit of the Earth (Isaiah 4:2)

Fruit of Thy Womb (Luke 1:42)

Fullers' Soap (Malachi 3:2)

Gift of God (John 4:10)

Gin (Isaiah 8:14)

Glorious High Throne from the
Beginning (Jeremiah 17:12)

Glorious Name (Isaiah 63:14)

Glory (Psalm 3:3; Haggai 2:7)

Glory as of the Only Begotten
of the Father (John 1:14)

Glory of God (Romans 3:23)

Glory of His Father
(Matthew 16:27; Mark 8:38)

God (Revelation 21:7)

God Blessed Forever
(Romans 9:5)

God Forever and ever
(Psalm 48:14)

God in the Midst of Her (Psalm
46:5)

God Manifest in the Flesh
(1 Timothy 3:16)

God of Glory (Psalm 29:3)

God of Israel (Psalm 59:5)

God of Jacob (Psalm 46:7)

God of My Life (Psalm 42:8)

God of My Mercy
(Psalm 59:10)

God of My Righteousness
(Psalm 4:1)

God of My Salvation
(Psalm 18:46; 24:5)

God of My Strength
(Psalm 43:2)

God Who Avengeth Me
(Psalm 18:47)

God Who Forgavest Them
(Psalm 99:8)

God with Us (Matthew 1:23)

Good Man (John 7:12)

Good Master (Matthew 19:16)

Good Shepherd (John 10:11)

Goodman of the House
(Matthew 20:11)

Governor Among Nations
(Psalm 22:28)

Great (Jeremiah 32:18)

Great God (Titus 2:13)

Great High Priest
(Hebrews 4:14)

Great Light (Isaiah 9:2)

Great Prophet (Luke 7:16)

Great Shepherd of the Sheep
(Hebrews 13:20)

Greater (1 John 4:4)

Greater and More Perfect
Tabernacle (Hebrews 9:11)

Greater than Jonah
(Matthew 12:41)

Greater than Our Father
Abraham (John 8:53, 57-58)

Greater than Our Father Jacob
(John 4:12)

Greater than Solomon
(Matthew 12:42)

Greater than the Temple
(Matthew 12:6)

Guest (Luke 19:7)

Guide Even unto Death
(Psalm 48:14)

Guide of My Youth
(Jeremiah 3:4)

Guiltless (Matthew 12:7)

Habitation of Justice
(Jeremiah 50:7)

Harmless (Hebrews 7:26;
"Blameless," NLT)

He Goat (Proverbs 30:31)

Head of All Principality and
Power (Colossians 2:10)

Head of Every Man
(1 Corinthians 11:3)

Head of the Body
(Colossians 1:18)

Head of the Corner
(1 Peter 2:7)

Health of My Countenance
(Psalm 42:11)

Heir (Mark 12:7)

Heir of All Things
(Hebrews 1:2)

Helper of the Fatherless
(Psalm 10:14)

Hen (Matthew 23:37)

Hidden Manna
(Revelation 2:17)

Hiding Place (Psalm 32:7)

Hiding Place from the Wind
(Isaiah 32:2)

High and Lofty One Who
Inhabiteth Eternity
(Isaiah 57:15)

High Priest (Hebrews 5:5)

High Priest After the Order of
Melchizedek (Hebrews 5:10)

High Priest Forever
(Hebrews 6:20)

High Tower (Psalm 18:2)

Highest Himself (Psalm 87:5)

Highway (Isaiah 35:8)

Holy (Isaiah 57:15)

Holy Child Jesus (Acts 4:27;
"Holy Servant," NKJV)

Holy One (Acts 2:27)

Holy One and Just (Acts 3:14)

Holy One of Israel
(Psalm 89:18)

Holy thing Which shall Be
Born of Thee (Luke 1:35)

Holy to the Lord (Luke 2:23)

Hope (1 Timothy 1:1)

Hope of Glory
(Colossians 1:27)

Hope of His People (Joel 3:16)

Hope of Israel (Acts 28:20)

Hope of Their Fathers
(Jeremiah 50:7)

Horn of David (Psalm 132:17)

Horn of Salvation (Luke 1:69)

Horn of the House of Israel
(Ezekiel 29:21)

House of Defense (Psalm 31:2)

Householder (Matthew 20:1)

Husband (Revelation 21:2)

I AM (John 18:6)

Image of the Invisible God
(Colossians 1:15)

Immanuel (Isaiah 7:14)

Innocent Blood
(Matthew 27:4)

Intercessor (Hebrews 7:24-25)

Isaac (Hebrews 11:17-18)

Jasper Stone (Revelation 4:3)

Jeremiah (Matthew 16:14)

Jesus (Matthew 1:21)

Jesus Christ (Hebrews 13:8)

Jesus Christ the Lord
(Romans 7:25)

Jesus Christ, the Son of God
(John 20:31)

Jesus of Galilee
(Matthew 26:69)

Jesus of Nazareth (John 1:45)

Jesus of Nazareth, the King of
the Jews (John 19:19)

Jew (John 4:9)

John the Baptist
(Matthew 16:14)

Joseph's Son (Luke 4:22)

Judge of the Quick and the
Dead (Acts 10:42; "Judge of the
Living and the Dead," *NKJV*)

Judge of the Widows
(Psalm 68:5)

Just One (Acts 7:52)

Just Person (Matthew 27:24)

Keeper (Psalm 12:15)

Kindness and Love of God
(Titus 3:4)

King Eternal (1 Timothy 1:17)

King Forever and Ever
(Psalm 10:16)

King Immortal
(1 Timothy 1:17)

King in His Beauty
(Isaiah 33:17)

King Invisible (1 Timothy 1:17)

King of All the Earth
(Psalm 47:7)

King of Glory (Psalm 24:7-8)

King of Heaven (Daniel 4:37)

King of Israel (John 1:49)

King of Kings and Lord of
Lords (Revelation 19:16)

King of Peace (Hebrews 7:2)

King of Righteousness
(Hebrews 7:2)

King of Saints
(Revelation 15:3)

King of Salem (Hebrews 7:2)

King of Terrors (Job 18:14)

King of the Jews (Matthew 2:2)

King Who Cometh in the
Name of the Lord (Luke 19:38)

King's Son (Psalm 72:1)

Kinsman (Ruth 4:14)

Ladder (Genesis 28:12)

Lamb (Revelation 17:14)

Lamb of God (John 1:29)

Lamb Slain from the Foundation of the World (Revelation 13:8)

Lamb That Was Slain (Revelation 5:12)

Lamb Who Is in the Midst of the Throne (Revelation 7:17)

Last (Isaiah 44:6)

Last Adam (1 Corinthians 15:45)

Lawgiver (James 4:12)

Leader (Isaiah 55:4)

Life (John 14:6)

Life-Giving Spirit (1 Corinthians 15:45)

Lifter Up of Mine Head (Psalm 3:3)

Light (John 1:7)

Light of the City (Revelation 21:23)

Light of the Glorious Gospel of Christ (2 Corinthians 4:4)

Light of the Knowledge of the Glory of God (2 Corinthians 4:6)

Light of Men (John 1:4)

Light of the Morning (2 Samuel 23:4)

Light of the World (John 8:12)

Light of Truth (Psalm 43:3)

Light to Lighten Gentiles (Luke 2:32)

Light to the Gentiles (Isaiah 49:6)

Lily Among thorns (Song of Solomon 2:2)

Lily of the Valleys (Song of Solomon 2:1)

Lion of the Tribe of Judah (Revelation 5:5)

Living Bread (John 6:51)

Living God (Psalm 42:2)

Lord (*despotes*; 2 Peter 2:1)

Lord (*kurios*; John 13:13)

Lord (*rabboni*; Mark 10:51)

Lord Also of the Sabbath
(Mark 2:28)

Lord and My God (John 20:28)

Lord and Savior (2 Peter 1:11)

Lord Both of the Dead and
Living (Romans 14:9)

Lord from Heaven
(1 Corinthians 15:47)

Lord God Almighty (Revelation
16:7)

Lord God of Israel
(Psalm 41:13)

Lord God of the Holy Prophets
(Revelation 22:6)

Lord God of Truth
(Psalm 41:13)

Lord God Omnipotent
(Revelation 19:6)

Lord God Who Judgeth Her
(Revelation 18:8)

Lord Holy and True (Revelation
6:10)

Lord Jesus (Romans 10:9)

Lord Jesus Christ (James 2:1)

Lord of All the Earth
(Joshua 3:11)

Lord of Glory
(1 Corinthians 2:8)

Lord of Hosts (Psalm 24:10)

Lord of Lords (1 Timothy 6:15)

Lord of Peace
(2 Thessalonians 3:16)

Lord of the Vineyard
(Matthew 20:8)

Lord of the Whole Earth
(Psalm 97:5)

Lord Our God (Psalm 8:1,9)

Lord Strong and Mighty (Psalm
24:8)

Lord Who Is and Who Was
and Who Is to Come
(Revelation 1:8, *NKJV*)

Lord's Christ
(Revelation 11:15)

Lord's Doing (Matthew 21:42)

Lowly in Heart
(Matthew 11:29)

Magnified (Psalm 40:16)

Maker (Psalm 95:6)

Malefactor (John 18:30)

Man (John 19:5)

Man Approved of God
(Acts 2:22)

Man Child (Revelation 12:5)

Man Christ Jesus
(1 Timothy 2:5)

Man Gluttonous
(Matthew 11:19)

Man of Sorrows (Isaiah 53:3)

Man Whom He Hath
Ordained (Acts 17:31)

Man Whose Name Is the
Branch (Zechariah 6:12)

Manna (Exodus 16:15)

Marvelous in Our Eyes
(Matthew 21:42)

Master
(didaskalos; John 11:28)

Master (epistates; Luke 5:5)

Master
(Kathegetes; Matthew 23:10)

Master (rabbi; John 4:31)

Master of the House
(oikodespotes; Luke 13:25)

Meat Offering (Leviticus 2:1)

Mediator (1 Timothy 2:5)

Mediator of a Better Covenant
(Hebrews 8:6)

Mediator of the New Covenant
(Hebrews 12:24)

Mediator of the New Testament
(Hebrews 9:15)

Meek (Matthew 11:29)

Melchizedek (Genesis 14:18)

Merciful and Faithful High
Priest (Hebrews 2:17)

Mercy and His Truth
(Psalm 57:3)

Mercy Seat
(Hebrews 9:5; 1 John 2:2)

Messenger of the Covenant
(Malachi 3:1)

Messiah (Daniel 9:26)

Messiah the Prince
(Daniel 9:25)

Mighty (Psalm 89:19)

Mighty God (Isaiah 9:6)

Mighty One of Jacob
(Isaiah 49:26; 60:16)

Minister of Sin
(Galatians 2:17)

Minister of the Circumcision
(Romans 15:8)

Minister of the Heavenly
Sanctuary (Hebrews 8:1-3)

More Excellent Name (Hebrews
1:4)

Morning Star (Revelation 2:28)

Most High (Psalm 9:2; 21:7)

Mouth of God (Matthew 4:4)

Mystery of God
(Colossians 2:2)

Nail Fastened in a Sure Place
(Isaiah 22:23)

Name Above Every Name
(Philippians 2:9)

Name for Salvation
(John 20:31)

Name No Man Knew
(Revelation 19:12)

Name of Jesus
(Colossians 3:17)

Nazarene (Matthew 2:23)

New Name (Revelation 3:12)

Nourisher of Thine Old Age
(Ruth 4:15)

Offering and a Sacrifice to God
(Ephesians 5:2)

Offspring of David
(Revelation 22:16)

Ointment Poured Forth
(Song of Solomon 1:3)

Omega (Revelation 22:13)

One of the Prophets
(Matthew 16:14)

Only Begotten of the Father
(John 1:14)

Only Begotten Son (John 3:16)

Only Potentate
(1 Timothy 6:15)

Only Wise God
(1 Timothy 1:17)

Owl of the Desert
(Psalm 102:6)

Passover (1 Corinthians 5:7)

Path of Life (Psalm 16:11)

Pavilion (Psalm 31:20)

Peace (Ephesians 2:14)

Peace Offering (Leviticus 3:1)

Pelican of the Wilderness
(Psalm 102:6)

Perfect Man (James 3:2)

Person of Christ
(2 Corinthians 2:10)

Physician (Luke 4:23)

Place of Our Sanctuary
(Jeremiah 17:12)

Place of Refuge (Isaiah 4:6)

Plant of Renown
(Ezekiel 34:29)

Polished Staff (Isaiah 49:2)

Poor (2 Corinthians 8:9)

Portion (Psalm 119:57)

Portion of Jacob
(Jeremiah 51:19)

Portion of Mine Inheritance
(Psalm 16:5)

Potter (Jeremiah 18:6)

Power of God
(1 Corinthians 1:24)

Praying in My Name
(John 14:14)

Precious (1 Peter 2:7)

Precious Cornerstone
(Isaiah 28:16)

Preeminence (Colossians 1:18)

Price (1 Corinthians 6:20)

Price of His Redemption
(Leviticus 25:52)

Priest Forever (Psalm 110:4)

Priest of the Most High God
(Hebrews 7:1)

Prince and Savior (Acts 5:31)

Prince of Life (Acts 3:15)

Prince of Peace (Isaiah 9:6)

Prince of Princes (Daniel 8:25)

Prince of the Kings of the Earth
(Revelation 1:5)

Prophet (John 7:40)

Prophet Mighty in Deed and
Word (Luke 24:19)

Prophet of Nazareth
(Matthew 21:11)

Prophet Without Honor
(Matthew 13:57)

Propitiation (1 John 2:1-2)

Pure (1 John 3:3)

Purifier of Silver (Malachi 3:3)

Quick Understanding
(Isaiah 11:3)

Quickening Spirit
(1 Corinthians 15:45)

Rabbi (John 3:2)

Rabboni (John 20:16)

Rain Upon the Mown Grass
(Psalm 72:6)

Ransom for All (1 Timothy 2:6)

Ransom for Many
(Matthew 20:28)

Red Heifer Without Spot
(Numbers 19:2)

Redeemer (Job 19:25)

Redemption (1 Corinthians
1:30; Luke 21:28)

Redemption of Their Souls
(Psalm 49:8)

Refiner's Fire (Malachi 3:2)

Refuge (Psalm 46:1)

Refuge for the Oppressed
(Psalm 9:9)

Refuge from the Storm
(Isaiah 25:4)

Refuge in Times of Trouble
(Psalm 9:9)

Report (Isaiah 53:1)

Reproach of Men (Psalm 22:6)

Resting Place (Jeremiah 50:6)

Restorer of Thy Life
(Ruth 4:15)

Resurrection (John 11:25)

Revelation of Jesus Christ
(Revelation 1:1)

Reverend (Psalm 111:9)

Reward for the Righteous
(Psalm 58:11)

Rich (Romans 10:12)

Riches of His Glory
(Romans 9:23)

Riddle (Judges 14:14)

Right (Deuteronomy 32:4)

Righteous (1 John 2:1)

Righteous Branch
(Jeremiah 23:5)

Righteous God (Psalm 7:9)

Righteous Judge
(2 Timothy 4:8)

Righteous Lord (Psalm 11:7)

Righteous Man (Luke 23:47)

Righteous Servant
(Isaiah 53:11)

Righteousness
(1 Corinthians 1:30)

Righteousness of God (Romans
10:3)

River of Water in a Dry Place
(Isaiah 32:2)

Rock (Matthew 16:18)

Rock of His Salvation
(Deuteronomy 32:15)

Rock of Israel (2 Samuel 23:3)

Rock of My Refuge
(Psalm 94:22)

Rock of Offense (Romans 9:33)

Rock of Our Salvation
(Psalm 95:1)

Rock of Spiritual Refreshment
(1 Corinthians 10:4, *TLB*)

Rock of Thy Strength
(Isaiah 17:10)

Rock That Is Higher than I
(Psalm 61:2)

Rod (Micah 6:9)

Rod out of the Stem of Jesse
(Isaiah 11:1)

Root and Offspring of David
(Revelation 22:16)

Root of David
(Revelation 5:5)

Root of Jesse
(Isaiah 11:10; Romans 15:12)

Root out of Dry Ground
(Isaiah 53:2)

Rose of Sharon
(Song of Solomon 2:1)

Ruler (Micah 5:2)

Sacrifice for Sins
(Hebrews 10:12)

Sacrifice to God
(Ephesians 5:2)

Salvation (Psalm 27:1)

Salvation of God
(Luke 2:30; 3:6)

Salvation of Israel
(Jeremiah 3:23)

Samaritan (John 8:48)

Same Yesterday, Today and
Forever (Hebrews 13:8)

Saviour (Titus 2:13)

Saviour of All Men
(1 Timothy 4:10)

Saviour of the Body
(Ephesians 5:23)

Saviour of the World
(John 4:42; 1 John 4:14)

Scapegoat
(Leviticus 16:8; John 11:49-52)

Sceptre of Israel
(Numbers 24:17)

Sceptre of Thy Kingdom (Psalm
45:6)

Second Man
(1 Corinthians 15:47)

Secret (Judges 13:18)

Secret of Thy Presence
(Psalm 31:20)

Seed of Abraham
(Galatians 3:16)

Seed of David
(Romans 1:3; 2 Timothy 2:8)

Seed of the Woman
(Genesis 3:15)

Sent One (John 9:4)

Separate from His Brethren
(Genesis 49:26)

Separate from Sinners (Hebrews
7:26)

Serpent in the Wilderness
(John 3:14)

Servant (Isaiah 42:1)

Servant of Rulers (Isaiah 49:7)

Servant the Branch
(Zechariah 3:8)

Shadow from the Heat
(Isaiah 25:4)

Shadow of a Great Rock (Isaiah
32:2)

Shadow of the Almighty (Psalm
91:1)

Shelter (Psalm 61:3)

Shepherd
(Psalm 23:1; Isaiah 40:11)

Shepherd of Israel (Psalm 80:1)

Shield (Psalm 84:9)

Shiloh (Genesis 49:10)

Shoshannim
(titles of Psalm 45; 69)

Sign of the Lord (Isaiah 7:11)

Siloam (John 9:7)

Sin (2 Corinthians 5:21)

Snare to the Inhabitants of
Jerusalem (Isaiah 8:14)

Son (Matthew 11:27)

Son from Heaven
(1 Thessalonians 1:10)

Son Given (Isaiah 9:6)

Son of Abraham (Matthew 1:1)

Son of David (Mark 10:47)

Son of God (John 1:49)

Son of Joseph (John 1:45)

Son of Man (John 1:51)

Son of Mary (Mark 6:3)

Son of the Blessed
(Mark 14:61)

Son of the Father (2 John 3)

Son of the Freewoman
(Galatians 4:30)

Son of the Highest (Luke 1:32)

Son of the Living God
(Matthew 16:16)

Son of the Most High
(Mark 5:7)

Son over His Own House
(Hebrews 3:6)

Son Who Is Consecrated for
Evermore (Hebrews 7:28)

Son (Isaiah 12:2)

Sower (Matthew 13:4, 37)

Sparrow Alone upon the House
Top (Psalm 102:7)

Spiritual Rock
(1 Corinthians 10:4)

Star out of Jacob (Numbers
24:17)

Stay (Psalm 18:18)

Stone Cut out of the Mountain
(Daniel 2:45)

Stone Cut Without Hands
(Daniel 2:34)

Stone of Israel (Genesis 49:24)

Stone of Stumbling
(1 Peter 2:8)

Stone Which the Builders
Refused (Psalm 118:22)

Stone Which the Builders
Rejected (Matthew 21:42)

Stone Which Was Set at
Nought (Acts 4:11)

Stranger (Matthew 25:35)

Strength (Isaiah 12:2)

Strength of Israel
(1 Samuel 15:29)

Strength of My Life
(Psalm 27:1)

Strength to the Needy in
Distress (Isaiah 25:4)

Strength to the Poor
(Isaiah 25:4)

Strong (Psalm 24:8)

Strong Consolation
(Hebrews 6:18)

Strong Lord (Psalm 89:8)

Strong Refuge (Psalm 71:7)

Strong Rock (Psalm 31:2)

Strong Tower (Proverbs 18:10)

Strong Tower from the Enemy
(Psalm 61:3)

Stronger than He (Luke 11:22)

Stronghold in the Day of
Trouble (Nahum 1:7)

Stumbling Block
(1 Corinthians 1:23)

Sun of Righteousness
(Malachi 4:2)

Sure Foundation (Isaiah 28:16)

Sure Mercies of David
(Isaiah 55:3; Acts 13:34)

Surety of a Better Testament
(Hebrews 7:22; "Surety of a
Better Covenant," *NKJV*)

Sweet-Smelling Savor
(Ephesians 5:2; "Sweet-Smelling
Aroma," *NKJV*)

Tabernacle for a Shadow (Isaiah
4:6)

Tabernacle of God
(Revelation 21:3)

Teacher (Matthew 10:25)

Teacher Come from God
(John 3:2)

Temple (John 2:19)

Tender Grass (2 Samuel 23:4)

Tender Mercy of God
(Luke 1:78)

Tender Plant (Isaiah 53:2)

Testator (Hebrews 9:16-17)

Testimony of God
(1 Corinthians 2:1)

The Christ (1 John 5:1)

Treasure (2 Corinthians 4:7)

Trespass Offering
(Leviticus 5:6)

Tried Stone (Isaiah 28:16)

Triumphant Lamb
(Revelation 5:6)

Triumphant Son of Man
(Revelation 1:12-13)

True Bread from Heaven
(John 6:32)

True God (Jeremiah 10:10)

True Light (John 1:9)

True Vine (John 15:1)

True Witness (Proverbs 14:25)

Trustworthy Witness
(Revelation 1:5, *MLB*)

Truth (John 14:6)

Undefiled (Hebrews 7:26)

Understanding (Proverbs 3:19)

Unspeakable Gift
(2 Corinthians 9:15)

Upholder of All Things
(Hebrews 1:3)

Upright (Psalm 92:15)

Urim and Thummin
(Exodus 28:30)

Veil (Hebrews 10:20)

Very Great (Psalm 104:1)

Very Present Help in Trouble
(Psalm 46:1)

Victory (1 Corinthians 15:54)

Vine (John 15:5)

Voice (Revelation 1:12)

Wall of Fire (Zechariah 2:5)

Wave Offering (Leviticus 7:30)

Way (John 14:6)

Way of Holiness (Isaiah 35:8)

Weakness of God
(1 Corinthians 1:25)

Wedding Garment
(Matthew 22:12)

Well of Salvation (Isaiah 12:3)

Wisdom (1 Corinthians 1:25)

Wisdom of God
(1 Corinthians 1:24)

Wise Master Builder
(1 Corinthians 3:10)

Witness (Judges 11:10)

Witness (Job 16:19)

Witness to the People
(Isaiah 55:4)

Wonderful (Isaiah 9:6)

Wonderful Counselor
(Isaiah 9:6)

Word (John 1:1)

Word of God (Revelation 19:13)
Word of Life (1 John 1:1)

Worm and No Man
(Psalm 22:6)

Worthy (Revelation 4:11; 5:12)

Worthy Name (James 2:7)

Worthy to Be Praised
(Psalm 18:3)

X (an unknown quantity; see
Revelation 19:12)

Yokefellow (Matthew 11:29-30)

Young Child (Matthew 2:11)

Zephnath-Paaneah
(Genesis 41:45)

Zeal of the Lord of Hosts
(Isaiah 37:32)

Zeal of Thine House
(Psalm 69:9; John 2:17)

Zerubbabel (Zechariah 4:7,9)

Appendix 6: The Names, Titles and Emblems Of the Holy Spirit

Anointing (1 John 2:27)

Another Helper (John 14:16)

Blessing (Isaiah 44:3)

Breath (Ezekiel 37:9)

Breath of God (Job 27:3)

Breath of Life
(Revelation 11:11)

Breath of the Almighty
(Job 33:4)

Breath of the LORD
(Isaiah 40:7)

Breath of Your Nostrils
(Psalm 18:15)

Deposit (2 Corinthians 1:22)

Dew (Hosea 14:5)

Different Spirit
(Numbers 14:24)

Divided Tongues, as of Fire
(Acts 2:3)

Door-Keeper (John 10:3, *NEB*)

Dove (Mark 1:10)

Down Payment
(see Ephesians 1:13-14)

Enduement of Power
(see Luke 24:49)

Eternal Spirit (Hebrews 9:14)

Excellent Spirit (Daneil 5:12)

Finger of God (Luke 11:20)

Floods on the Dry Ground
(Isaiah 44:3)

Fountain of Water (John 4:14)

Fullness of God
(Ephesians 3:19)

Gatekeeper (John 10:3, *RSV*)

Generous Spirit (Psalm 51:12)

Gift of God
(John 4:10; Acts 8:20)

Gift of the Holy Spirit
(Acts 2:38)

Glory of the Lord
(2 Corinthians 3:18)

God (Acts 5:4)

Good Spirit (Nehemiah 9:20)

Guarantee of Our Inheritance
(Ephesians 1:14; see 2
Corinthians 5:5)

Hand of God (2 Chron. 30:12)

Hand of the LORD (Job 12:9;
Isaiah 41:20)

Hand of the Lord GOD
(Ezekiel 8:1)

He/Himself (John 14:16,26;
Romans 8:16,26)

Helper (John 14:26)

His Holy One (Isaiah 10:17)

His Holy Spirit (Isaiah 63:10)

His Spirit (Numbers 11:29)

Holy One (Job 6:10)

Holy Spirit (Luke 11:13)

Holy Spirit of God
(Ephesians 4:30)

Holy Spirit of Promise
(Ephesians 1:13)

Holy Spirit Sent from Heaven
(1 Peter 1:12)

Holy Spirit Who Dwells in Us
(2 Timothy 1:14)

Holy Spirit Who Is in You
(1 Corinthians 6:19)

Lord (2 Corinthians 3:17)

Lord of the Harvest
(Matthew 9:38)

Mighty Voice (Psalm 68:33)

My Spirit (Genesis 6:3)

New Spirit (Ezekiel 11:19)

Oil (Hebrews 1:9)

Oil of Gladness
(Psalm 45:7; Hebrews 1:9)

One Spirit (1 Corinthians
12:13; Ephesians 2:18; 4:4)

Power of the Highest
(Luke 1:35)

Promise (Acts 2:39)

Promise of My Father
(Luke 24:49)

Promise of the Father
(Acts 1:4)

Promise of the Holy Spirit
(Acts 2:33)

Promise of the Spirit (Galatians
3:14)

Rain (Psalm 72:6)

Rivers of Living Water
(John 7:38)

Same Spirit
(1 Corinthians 12:4, 8-9, 11)

Same Spirit of Faith
(2 Corinthians 4:13)

Seal
(John 6:27; 2 Timothy 2:19)

Seal of God (Revelation 9:4)

Seal of the Living God
(Revelation 7:2)

Seed (1 John 3:9)

Seven Eyes (Zechariah 3:9;
4:10; Revelation 5:6)

Seven Horns (Revelation 5:6)

Seven Lamps of Fire Burning
Before the Throne
(Revelation 4:5)

Seven Spirits of God
(Revelation 3:1; 4:5)

Seven Spirits of God Sent Out
into All the Earth
(Revelation 5:6)

Seven Spirits Who Are Before
His Throne (Revelation 1:4)

Showers That Water the Earth
(Psalm 72:6)

Sound from Heaven (Acts 2:2)

Spirit (Numbers 27:18)

Spirit of A Sound Mind
(2 Timothy 1:7)

Spirit Who Dwells in You
(Romans 8:11)

Spirit Who Is from God
(1 Corinthians 2:12)

Spirit Whom He Has Given Us
(1 John 3:24)

Steadfast Spirit (Psalm 51:10)

Voice (Psalm 95:7; Hebrews 3:7)

Voice of the Almighty
(Ezekiel 1:24)

Voice of the LORD
(Psalm 29:3-5,7-9)

Voice of Thunder (Psalm 77:18)

Water (Isaiah 44:3)

Well of Living Waters
(John 4:14)

Wind (John 3:8)

Wisdom of His Spirit
(Ephesians 1:17)

Witness
(Job 16:19; Hebrews 10:15)

Your Holy Spirit (Psalm 51:11)

Your Spirit (Psalm 104:30)
Source: Elmer L. Towns, *The Names of Jesus* (Denver, CO: Accent Publications, 1987).

Appendix 7:
Trail of Manuscripts Leading to the King James Bible
Presented by Carl Baugh Ph.D.
Founder and Director of Creation Evidence Museum

The influence of the King James Bible cannot be totally appreciated, adequately comprehended, or fully defined. As the beautiful and purified translation of the original Hebrew and Greek languages, this text arrived on the scene of human history as the English Language itself was becoming standardized. The very words, phrases, and melodic patterns of the text became a part of the English Culture, and fanned the flames of freedom in the hearts of oppressed peoples on multiple continents. This Book has stirred the emotions of impassioned pulpiteers and comforted the spirits of dying saints. It has controlled the distempers of monarchs and consoled the plight of paupers. The King James Bible has enveloped entire civilizations in its mantle. Its message has populated Heaven and altered the course of Earth's history.

Referring to an original 1611 edition copy, Moira Goff of the British Library said of the *King James Bible*, "I think we have to be very careful in looking at the Bible only as a work of literature. It is also the Holy Scripture, and I think that makes it a different sort of book than the great works of literature. [It is] so embedded in us that we can't overstate the significance of it...its influence has been greater than that of Shakespeare."

Numerous scholars involved in scientific research echo similar sentiments, "There is no doubt that God providentially used King James to initiate what is likely the greatest translation project in history – one that brought the Word of God to multiplied millions of English-speaking people around the world" (ICR *Acts & Facts*, April 2011). We cannot overlook the fact that this 400-year-old Translation standardized the English Language, the language that became the common means of communication among all modern nations.

The Creation Evidence Museum of Glen Rose, Texas is in receipt of a very rare and valuable *1521 Gerbelius Greek New Testament*–as well as a trail of manuscripts leading ultimately to the *King James Bible* itself. This unique 500-year-old edition was edited by Nicolas Gerbelius, assistant to Desiderius Erasmus, the primary scholar responsible for the compilation of various handwritten *Greek New Testament* manuscripts into the first printed versions of the Greek text. In the natural course of correcting type-setting errors, and including all the properly preserved passages (such as the "Comma Johanneum" verse in 1 John 5:7), the Erasmus Greek Text became recognized in 1633 as the *Textus Receptus,* the *Received Text* – the preserved Word of God. The *1521 Gerbelius Greek New Testament* was, by all indications, an intermediate proof text, a vital link in the chain of man-uscripts.

This priceless volume was purchased and made possible by a special *heritage gift* from the Co-author of *Search the Scriptures for Yourself,* Geraldine Marquis-Combs Ph.D.

To understand the significance of this unique 1521manuscript, we must first understand some of the background surrounding the profound scholar and able translator, Desiderius Erasmus. Encyclopedia Wikipedia relates the following:

> **Novum Instrumentum omne** (Latin for *The New Instrument,* or *The New Testament*) was the first published *New Testament* in Greek (1516). It was prepared by Desiderius Erasmus (1469–1536) and printed by Johann Froben (1460–1527) of Basel. This new work was given the characteristically long name of *Novum Instrumentum omne, diligenter ab Erasmo Rot. Recognitum et Emendatum.* The second edition used the more familiar term *Testamentum* instead of *Instrumentum.* Erasmus used several Greek manuscripts housed in Basel, but some passages he translated from the Latin Vulgate. The second edition (1519) became the basis for Luther's German translation.
>
> Five editions of *Novum Instrumentum omne* were published. Of these four and five were not regarded as being so important as the third edition (1522), which was used by William Tyndale in the publication of the first *English New Testament* (1526) and later by translators of the *Geneva Bible* and the *King James Bible.* With the third edition, the "Comma Johanneum" was included. The Erasmian edition was the basis for the majority of modern

translations of the *New Testament* in the 16–19th centuries.

Popular demand for *Greek New Testaments* led to a flurry of further authorized and unauthorized editions in the ensuing sixteenth century; almost all of which were based on Erasmus' work and incorporated his particular readings.

Biblical Chronologist Floyd Nolen Jones reports that...

in 1624, Bonaventure and Abraham Elzevir, two brothers and printers, at Leiden of Holland produced a Greek New Testament edition. The origin of the term "Textus Receptus" comes from the publisher's preface to the 1633 edition. There, the Latin reads: *textum ergo habes, nunc ab omnibus receptum, in quo nihil immulatum aut corruptum damus*, meaning: "so you hold the text, now received by all, in which nothing corrupt." The two words, *textum* and *receptum*, were modified from the accusative to the nominative case to render *textus receptus* which means the "Received Text" (i.e., received from God). The Elzevir brothers said they had not altered the manuscripts in any way and that they considered the text in their hands to have been received directly from God.

The second Elzevir edition (1633) was generally adopted as the *Textus Receptus* on the European Continent whereas England came to consider the 1550 third edition of Stephanus as the standard "received text." All of these men believed they were working with the infallible Words of God as He had given them.[1] Over time, the term *Textus Receptus* has been retroactively applied to Erasmus' editions, as his work served as the basis of the others.[2]

The *1521 Erasmus Greek New Testament* was edited by Nicolas Gerbelius, Erasmus' colleague and sub-editor. This edition was the first "quarto" printing of the *Greek New Testament* of Erasmus; first printing of that text in any format smaller than the 1516 and 1519 small "folios;" and first separate printing of the text in any format. By "first separate printing" it is meant that this edition was the first printing of the *Greek New Testament* text without the Latin parallel text. Editions 1516 and 1519 included the parallel text in Latin on each page.

Even while Erasmus was still at work on his *Greek New Testament* and Latin re-translation, Nicholas Gerbelius, the editor of the edition at hand, wrote to him on 11 September 1515 to urge that the Greek should be printed separately for convenience (Tregelles, Account, p. 20). It has been suggested that it was this 1521 separate edition that Martin Luther actually worked from in translating his "September" New Testament of 1522.

The uniqueness of the particular mint-condition 1521 "proof copy" owned by the Creation Evidence Museum is apparent when we consider the following features. The original cover is not made of leather; instead, it has a hard cover bound with vellum, hand lettered in bold-colored Latin script. The Title Page is inscribed above the first printed line with a hand written Latin idiomatic notation, perhaps indicating the purpose and pattern of the ongoing inscriptions. Over 1,000 handwritten annotations in Greek, Latin, and Hebrew have been observed running throughout the volume. These annotations have been identified by the Linguistics Faculty of the Southwestern Baptist Theological Seminary as being of sixteenth century origin - that is, belonging to the same 1500's time period as the publication. The Greek text runs properly; yet, in eight different sections the page numbers are out of sequence. In two instances the numbers six and nine are exchanged. Such preliminary copies would hardly be available for public distribution. It is readily apparent that this particular first-run copy was probably used by the editor (or his assistants) as an "intermediate copy" in preparation for the 1522 edition that included the Comma Johanneum and other textual clarifications.

This thesis is supported by the fact that in this particular copy of the 1521 *Gerbelius Greek New Testament* one of the major idiomatic Latin annotations is placed in the margin of 1 John 5, next to the space where the Comma Johanneum was included in the forthcoming 1522 Erasmus edition. The Linguistics Faculty at SWBTS preliminarily translated part of the sixteenth-century idiomatic Latin abbreviated annotation as "enlarge the text." Dr. Dirk Obbink, Director of Ancient Language Studies at Oxford's ChristChurch Campus translated a part of the annotation as "Domini ipsissimi," "of the Lord himself." It appears that this is a notation to enlarge the text referring to "the Lord himself," that is, the Trinity passage known as Comma Johanneum, or 1 John 5:7.

What is the Comma Johanneum, and why is it so significant? In early Christian history Origen Adamantius (Origen of Alexander: c. 185-254) deliberately corrupted many of the Greek handwritten manuscripts by re-copying them and leaving out the pivotal deity passage in 1 John 5. This passage (v.7) reads: "For there are three that bear record in heaven, the Father, the Word, and the Holy Spirit, and these three are one." Since he did not believe in the full divinity of Christ, he corrupted this passage along with others. His corrupted manuscripts were not accepted by many of the local congregations; and consequently, a few of these manuscripts (such as the *Sinaiticus Aleph* and *Codex Vaticanus B*) were set aside–only to be "discovered" at a later time and survive among more "liberal" theologians in the centuries following.

It is to be remembered that the 1522 Third Edition of the *Erasmus Greek New Testament* provided the foundation for the *Geneva Bible* and the *King James Bible*. If our thesis is correct, we have in the margin of this 1521 volume a direct written request to include the "Johannine Trinity Statement" in the subsequent edition to be released the following year. The inclusion of 1 John 5:7 is "Domini ipsissimi - of the Lord himself," "for it pleased the Father that in Him should all fullness dwell" (Colossians 1:19).

****

The Trail of Manuscripts Leading to the King James Bible began with the beneficent reception of the intermediate 1521 *Gerbelius Greek New Testament*. The train of manuscripts that followed in rapid succession was staggering.

Beginning with the Old Testament, the Creation Evidence Museum recently received a priceless 400-year-old *Torah Scroll*. This Scroll consists of the *Books of Moses*, the first five books of the Bible. Originally hand-copied in Eastern Europe, this particular scroll has been in the custody of a beloved American Jewish family for many decades. It was on premise–being read by Jewish Rabbis at the Old Museum of Art in Tel Aviv, Israel–as David Ben Gurion announced the rebirth of the Nation of Israel. The Rabbis were reading Deuteronomy 28–30: the passage forecasting events to occur with Israel across the centuries, including God's promise to bring them back to their Land.

The museum holds a 250-year-old *Scroll of Esther* describing the attempt by Haman to obliterate the Jewish seed from the face of the Earth. The Scroll culminates with the preservation of the Hebrew people through the efforts of a brave Jewish woman. A 200-year-old Isaiah Scroll announces the hope of the world through the birth, life, death, burial, resurrection, and future kingdom of the Jewish Messiah–the son of a virgin. "His Name shall be called Wonderful, Counselor, the Mighty God, the Everlasting Father, and the Prince of Peace" (Isaiah 9:6).

The *Old* and *New Testaments* are bridged by two remarkable small amulets also owned by the museum. These amulets are pure gold and each features an outline of the Temple in Jerusalem, including the two front pillars. Being written in ancient Uncial Greek, the text is clear but idiomatic in its use of letters and words. A preliminary translation of the *first amulet* reads: "In the year of the raging waters of Noah the King roared." Apparently this is an abbreviated paraphrase of David's Psalm 29. A preliminary translation of the *second amulet* reads: "I am praying the Exceeding One John declared I will see." This may be an incredible prayer of faith stemming from the message of John the Baptist just before Jesus came on the public scene.

The trail of manuscripts pivots with the 1521 *Gerbelius Greek New Testament* described at length above.

Next is the 1531 *Basileas Greek New Testament*, a continuation of the manuscripts based upon the work of Erasmus.

This introduces the 1546 *Stephanus Greek New Testament*. Floyd Nolen Jones describes its significance:

> Robert Estienne, known as Stephanus (1503–1559), a printer from Paris, edited the Greek New Testament four times, in 1546, 1549, 1550 and 1551, the last in Geneva. The first two are among the neatest Greek texts known; the third edition is said to be a splendid masterpiece of typographical skill. The edition of 1551 contains the division of the New Testament into verses for the first time. The third edition of Stephanus (Estienne) was used by Theodore Beza (1519–1605), who edited it nine times between 1565 and 1604. In 1598, Beza published his fifth edition, again using Erasmus' Greek text as his foundation. Beza's fifth is the actual edition upon which the King James Bible was principally based.

The *1570 Erasmus Greek Nouum Testamentum* is encased in beautiful leather cover with brass clasps. This volume represents the crowning work of the man God used to compile the *Greek New Testament* from uncorrupted Greek manuscripts. As has been stated, his work provided the foundation for the *Geneva Bible* and the *King James Bible*. All other translators stand on his broad shoulders. Next is shown the *1588 Greek New Testament* published by Johanne Leusden, known as the "poor man's Bible." The cover and paper were of inferior stock, but publication of this New Testament provided the man on the street an opportunity to own a copy of God's Word.

Finally we present the 1609 *Judas Bible*. This particular edition of the *Geneva Bible* was corrupted by a typesetter. As was discussed previously, in early Christian history Origen of Alexandria deliberately corrupted handwritten copies of the Scriptures by omitting 1 John 5:7 and other passages. In the 1609 case the typesetter deliberately changed the single word "Jesus" to "Judas" in John 6:67. The passage should read, (v.67) "Then said Jesus unto the twelve, Will ye also go away? (v. 68) Then Simon Peter answered him, Lord, to whom shall we go? Thou hast the words of eternal life." In changing "Jesus" to "Judas" he negated the *Old Testament* prophesies and the validity of the earthly life of Christ. The typesetter was sentenced to jail by the king, and the printer suffered huge losses. All known copies of this edition were confiscated and destroyed. Very few copies remain, including this rare volume owned by the Creation Evidence Museum.

Footnotes:

[1]   How much do the editions differ over the span from 1550 to 1624? Elzevir differed from Stephenus, for example, in Mark only 19 times. Compare that with Codex Vaticanus B (a 4th century uncial MSS which is currently accepted as the most reliable, almost to the exclusion of all others, of the Greek manuscripts by most modern text critics). B differs with Sinaiticus Aleph (Hebrew designation = a) 652 times in the Gospel of Mark and with another uncial manuscript (D) in 1,944 places. In fact, there is only a total of 287 variants from Stephenus' 1550 work to the

Elzevir brothers' work of 1624. These few differences are almost negligible for they are all spelling. The issue becomes one of whether one spells "colour" or "color"?

Thus, the text has been protected by God. Again, God's preservation of the New Testament text was not by a miracle but providentially. It is not God-breathed and God inspired in the same exact sense that the "originals" were but it was, beyond all reasonable doubt, God guided and God-preserved.

2   [Bruce M. Metzger, Bart D. Ehrman, The Text Of The New Testament: Its Transmission, Corruption and Restoration, (Oxford University Press, 2005), p. 152]

Appendix 8: A Brief Outline of Bible Translations Presented by Mal Couch

The most significant translations of the Bible...

Codex Vaticanus
Date: A.D. 325
Contents: Septuagint Translation, Old and New Testaments
Language: Greek
Location: Vatican

Codex Sinaiticus
Date: A.D. 340
Contents: Septuagint Translation, Old and New Testaments
Language: Greek
Location: British Museum

Latin Vulgate ("Common" Translation)
Date: A.D. 385-405
Contents: Old and New Testaments
Translator: Jerome
Language: Latin
Location: Rome

Codex Alexandrinus
Date: A.D. 450
Contents: Old Testament (Septuagint), New Testament
Language: Greek
Location: British Museum

Codex Ephraemi Rescriptus
Date: A.D. 450
Language: Greek
Location: National Library, Paris

Pre-Reformation and Reformation Translations...

John Wycliffe's Bible
Date: New Testament completed in 1380; Old Testament completed in 1382
Translated from the Latin Vulgate
Language: Middle English mixed with Norman-French
Hand copied before the printing press; took 10 months to copy Wycliffe's Bible; cost: $200.00

Tyndale's Bible
Date: New Testament completed in 1525, portions of the Old Testament translated before his martyrdom
Language: English, first to be mass produced
Tyndale's Bible, though incomplete, was the first English Translation to work directly with the Hebrew and Greek texts

Erasmus' Greek New Testament and Latin Text
Date: 1516
Language: Greek, with Latin Vulgate Text
100,000 copies were sold in France alone
It is said to have caused "a great awakening and a desire for a good English translation from the Greek language."

Nicolas Gerbelius Greek New Testament
Date: 1521
Language: Greek
This Greek New Testament is understood to be an editor's intermediate text for qualifying and purifying the Greek source Texts. One special copy is known to contain approximately 1,000 sixteenth century annotations, preliminarily attributed to Gerbelius himself. Of special interest is the annotated request to include the "Comma Johannium" Trinity passage in 1 John 5 for "Domini Ipsissi" – "for God Himself."
Location: Creation Evidence Museum, Glen Rose, Texas

Coverdale's Bible
Date: 1539
It was also called the Cranmer, Whitchurch or Cromwell Bible. Seven editions were published between 1539-41. Earlier it had been forbidden, then tolerated, then licensed, then commanded to be read. This became the first

"Authorized" Bible, and Cromwell issued a royal proclamation commanding that it be read publicly in every church in England. King Henry accepted this Bible.

Taverner's Bible
Date: 1539
Translated by the Oxford Greek scholar, Richard Taverner

Geneva Bible
Date: 1560
Third revision of the Tyndale Bible. Introduction by John Calvin. This Bible was sanctioned by Knox, Calvin and Beza.

Bishop's Bible
Date: 1568
Fourth revision of the Tyndale Bible. A committee of eight bishops worked on this Bible, thus The Bishop's Bible. This cumbersome and costly Bible was not very popular.

King James Bible
Date: 1611
This was the fifth revision of the Tyndale Bible. When King James I became King of England (1603-25) he recognized that progress had been made regarding language scholarship. He knew that a refined Bible was needed to unite the English people. On July 22, 1604, a translation committee was formed with 54 Greek and Hebrew scholars. They finished the translation in three years, and the first edition was published in 1611.

Several revisions followed to correct errors in type, spelling and translation, notably those of 1615, 1629 and 1638. Three important additional revisions can be mentioned: (1) that of Bishop Lloyd (1701), in which the chronology of Archbishop Ussher was introduced; (2) that of Dr. Paris, Fellow of Trinity College (1762), the Cambridge Bible, introducing 383 marginal notes and other changes; (3) that of Dr. Blayney (1769), the Oxford Bible, introducing 76 changes, including many on weights, measures and coins. The object of these revisions was to restore the text of 1611, to modernize the language and spelling, to discard references to unparallel passages, to introduce new marginal references making clear the Hebrew-English-equivalent proper names, to clarify the use of italics, and to reform the punctuation.

The King James Bible has endeared itself to the hearts and lives of millions of Christians and has molded the characters of the leaders in every walk of life in the greatest nation of the world. During all these centuries the King James Bible has become a vital part of the English-speaking world, socially, morally, religiously and politically. Launched with the endorsement of the regal and scholarly authority of the 17th century, its conquest and rule have been supreme. No versions of private origin, even in the face of advances in scholarship, could compete with it.

-I. M. Price, *The Ancestry of our English Bible*

Right: Cover of Gerbelius Greek New Testament... The manuscript that started our current avalanche of blessing!

Left: 1570 Erasmus Greek New Testament (Textus Receptus)

ΕΠΙΣΤΟΛΗ

Top: Annotation beside 1 John 5 from the 1570 Erasmus Greek New Testament (Textus Receptus). Left: Close-up of annotation.

"Poor Man's Bible

Ἡ ΚΑΙΝΗ
ΔΙΑΘΗΚΗ.

NOVUM
TESTAMENTUM.

In quo non tantum selecti versica-
li 1900, continentes omnes voces
Novi T. asteriscis notantur, sed
etiam omnes & singulæ voces
semel vel sæpius occurrentes, di-
stinctâ notâ distinguuntur.

AUCTORE
JOHANNE LEUSDEN

AMSTELODAMI,
Apud HENRICUM & Viduam
THEODORI BOOM 1688.

JOHANNES LEUSDEN
Lectori Benevolo

S.

DIDERAM anno hujus
seculi septuagesimo quinto Novum Testamentum Græcum, in
quo versibus selectis mille &
nongentis (cum omnes versi-
culi Novi Testamenti sint septies mille non
genti quinquaginta novem) præfixeram
asteriscum: quia omnes & singulæ voces totius
Novi Testamenti, quæ sunt 4956, in annota-
tatis versiculis continentur. Illis exemplari-
bus diù distractis, jam in publicum emitto
alteram editionem, correctissimam, in qua non
tantum illis mille & nongentis versiculis aste-
riscus est præfixus, sed etiam omnibus & sin-
gulis vocibus Novi T. sive semel sive sæpius
occurrentibus, distincta notula est præposita.
Hâc notula (†) denotat vocem, cui ea præfi-
gitur, tantum semel, vel (si bis) in unico versi-
culo extareæquales voces in N.T. extant 1686.
Hac verò notula (‖) significat eam vocem,
cui ea præponitur, bis vel sæpius & in pluri-
bus versibus occurrere. Præterea in fine sin-
gulorum Capitum adduntur duplices notæ
numericæ, quarum priores exprimunt in gene-
re numerum vocum annotatarum, & semel vel
sæpius in illo Capite occurentium; posteriores
verò, quibus semper hæc notula (†) præponitur, exprimunt, voces semel tantum extantes:
ex.gr. in fine Capitis secundi Matthæi extant
* 2

Above: Title Page of "Poor Man's
Bible" Left: Introduction, "Poor
Man's Bible"

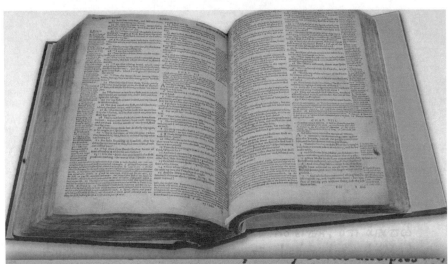

NICOLAVS

GERBELIVS CHRISTI
ANIS OMNIBVS
FOELICITA
TEM.

IHIL eſt in Chriſto Ieſu beni⁄
gniſſimo Seruatore noſtro, tam
puſillum, nihil tam tenui ſpecie,
quod non admiratione ſui oíum
in ſe animos poſſit allicere, quod
humanam métem in contempla
tione maieſtatis atꝗ gloriæ filii
Dei uelut abſorptam, non rapiat, inflammet, excitet.
Sed enim hoc unum, inter alia plæráꝗ, pro ingenii
mei tenuitate demirari ſoleo, Chriſtũ filium æterni
Dei, ſplendorem gloriæ & expreſſam illius imaginé,
tanta clemétia, tamꝗ admirabili benignitate, ſe ho
minũ adiunxiſſe imbecillitati, atꝗ eorum ſané qui
præter nominis humilitatem, nihil etiam alióqui li
berale, nihil ingenuum præ ſe ferebant. Primi erãt
oíñium paſtores ouium, pecoriſꝗ magiſtri, quos glo
ria domini circumfulſit. Piſcatores pari manſuetudi
ne, ad diuitias regni ſui prouocauit. Data opera trãſ
eo, qua ſe perpetuo lenitate, publicanis, nũmulariis,

ii

Top: Title Page of Gerbelius Greek New Testament with
introducing annotation at the top.
Previous page top: Judas Bible open to corrupted passage at
John 6:67. Middle: Close-up of Judas Bible corruption.
Bottom: Judas Bible cover.

Gold Amulets

Gold Amulets

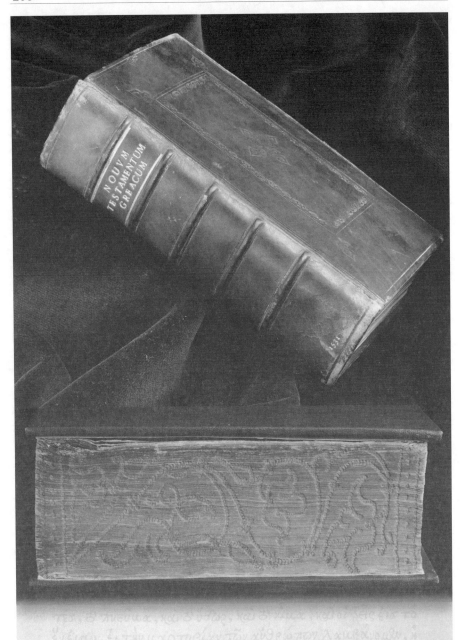

Top: 1531 Greek New Testament
Bottom:"Grafted" Edges of Stephanus New Testament
Next Page: Title Page to Stephanus' Greek New Testament

ΤΗΣ ΚΑΙΝΗΣ ΔΙΑΘΗ-
ΚΗΣ ΑΠΑΝΤΑ.

Nouum Testamentum.

EX BIBLIOTHECA REGIA.

Βασιλῇ τ' ἀγαθῷ κραιερῷ τ' αἰχμητῇ.

LVTETIAE.

Ex officina Roberti Stephani typographi
Regÿ, typis Regÿs.

M. D. XLVI.

ΤΗ͂Σ ΚΑΙΝΗ͂Σ ΔΙΑΘΗΚΗΣ ΆΠΑΝΤΑ,

Noui Teſtamenti omnia.

Illustrations at introduction to Stephanus' Greek New Testament

Stephanus' signature illustration in all of his editions

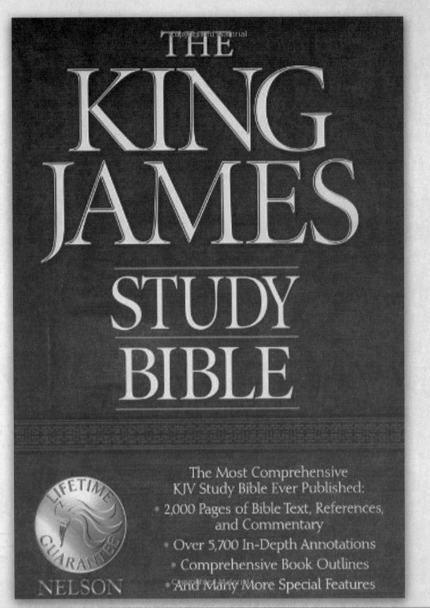

This classic King James Version Reference Bible has a wealth of study helps. Over 60,000 center-column references guide you to related verses for further study and understanding of the Bible, and a concordance enables you to locate key verses and concepts. Book introductions, explanatory notes, and full-color maps furnish background information to enhance understanding of the Scriptures.

JIM
ABOUT THE AUTHORS
COMBS

First enrolling as a freshman in January of 1946, James O. (Jim) Combs graduated with a diploma in 1951 and was one of the first four to receive the Bachelor of Arts in Biblical Education from Kansas City Bible College in 1952. During 1948-50, Combs, who was pastoring in Texas at the time, also completed a bachelor's degree in theology at the Bible Baptist Seminary in Fort Worth, before returning to Missouri. While in Fort Worth Jim participated in the founding of the Baptist Bible Fellowship International, the Baptist Bible College and the Baptist Bible Tribune, a weekly paper. He also attended Baptist Bible College and served as the second president of the BBC Alumni Association in 1960.

Ministering in California from 1953 until 1975, Jim also completed an MA through California Baptist Theological Seminary and Jackson College in Hawaii (1964). He earned a Doctor of Ministry from Louisiana Baptist University in 1985 and received an honorary Doctor of Literature in 1986 from Liberty University in Lynchburg, Virginia. Besides pastoring, Jim taught in Pacific Coast Baptist Bible College and at various times was on radio and television. From 1973-75 he served as president of the Western States Baptist Bible Fellowship.

Jim pastored for 26 years, mostly in California at one church in Lynwood and another in Costa Mesa (First Baptist Church); then ran for the United States Congress in 1976, winning the nomination of a major party in his California district. During his campaign, he and Jeri Marquis Combs were guests of President Gerald Ford at the White House.

From 1977 until the present he has been an evangelist and conference speaker, majoring on prophetic subjects. In 1982 he became editor of the Baptist Bible Tribune, published in Springfield, Missouri for the Baptist Bible Fellowship International (4,000 churches). Retiring from that post in 1995 he became founding Editor-in-Chief of Jerry Falwell's National Liberty Journal, serving for a year and a half.

He is the author or editor of several books, including *Mysteries of The Book of Daniel, Rainbows From Revelation, Mysteries of the Bible Now Revealed, Ten Tremendous Truths, Our Biblical Baptist Heritage* and *ABC's of*

Life Success by Jim and Jeri Combs. He is also an associate editor of the Tim LaHaye Prophecy Study Bible.

He has preached in hundreds of pulpits during his 65 years of ministry. He was also a Staley Lecturer.

Presently, he serves as Provost and a Mentoring Professor for Louisiana Baptist University and Louisiana Baptist Theological Seminary, based in Shreveport Louisiana.

He and Jeri reside in Springfield, Missouri.

EARLY LIFE

Jim was born October 6th, 1927, in Lubbock, Texas; was converted in 1940 through Charles E. Fuller's radio ministry; was baptized in 1943 at the First Baptist Church in San Antonio. He was licensed to preach on his 16th birthday by the Huisache Avenue Baptist Church of San Antonio. He began teaching a Bible class immediately and preached his first sermon October 31, 1943.

ACADEMIC DEGREES

Th.G.   Baptist Bible College 1952
B.A.   Calvary Bible College (KCBC) 1952
B.Div.   Bible Baptist Seminary 1950
M.A.   Jackson College 1965
M.Div.   Louisiana Baptist Theological Seminary 1991
D.Min.   Louisiana Baptist University 1985

HONORARIA
D.D.   California Graduate School of Theology 1984
Litt.D.   Liberty University 1986

JERI MARQUIS-COMBS

Jeri Marquis-Combs, shortly after she placed her faith in Christ, enrolled in Kansas City's Bible College's night classes in 1943. She also took courses at Central Baptist Theological Seminary. In 1945, she registered as a full time student at the new KCBC campus at 75th and State Line Road and became Dr. Walter L. Wilson's assistant secretary.

Graduating in 1948 with a missions diploma, she moved to Toronto, Canada to study at the Missionary Medical Institute. In 1950 she resumed her position with Dr. Wilson and graduated in 1952 with a Bachelor of Arts degree.

During her years at KCBC she was active in Child Evangelism Fellowship, Rural Bible Crusades and also, during her last two years in college, she taught the Criterion Adult Bible Class for business adults at the Country Club Congregational Church in Kansas City, Missouri.

She and Jim were married on May 27th at KCBC's Bulkley Auditorium in 1952 by Dr. Walter L Wilson, Jeri's pastor. They both graduated, receiving the first B.A. degrees offered by the college on May 30th,1952.

They served together at the Tabernacle Baptist Church in Joplin, Missouri (1952-53). Then they moved to California where they spent 17 years at the Olivet Baptist Church in Lynwood. She served as church secretary, Christian Education Director and a teacher or superintendent of every department in the Sunday School at various times. She also taught a large adult class in 1965.

Through classes taken at California Baptist Theological Seminary and Jackson College of Hawaii, she earned a Master of Religious Education in 1965.

Jeri was Christian Education Director of a branch congregation called Valley Baptist Church of Northridge in 1965-66, a position she later held at the First Baptist Church of Costa Mesa during their tenure there (1970-75).

Jeri traveled for several years with Jim in evangelism and prophecy conferences from coast to coast.

In 1983 they moved to Springfield, Missouri where Jim became editor of the Baptist Bible Tribune, official publication of the Baptist Bible Fellowship International. She was Family Page Editor.

They collaborated on several study projects and publishable books in recent years. During this time she completed a Master of Arts and a Doctorate in Counseling through Louisiana Baptist University. She is a founding charter member of the American Association of Christian Counselors.

Jim and Jeri have been married for 59 years and have one daughter, Charis Lorraine Combs-Lay, who is a Lutheran Minister, as is her husband, Leo. Charis also ministers at a Presbyterian Church in their town. They each hold degrees from Berkley, California. They have provided Jim and Jeri with two grandchildren, James Edward and Steven Charles.

Lee and Gerd Fredrickson, their chosen son and daughter, have three children. Anna Louise is married to Jonathan Saliba, and they are currently serving as missionaries in Bogata Columbia. Ingrid Elise is married to Cody Shores, and they are both studying for their masters degrees at Baptist Bible College, Springfield, Missouri, where Ingid works parttime. Cody is a minister at Seminole Baptist Tempe in Springfield, Missouri. Karl Donald is in his Junior year at Baptist Bible College where he is also in charge of media.

These two graduates testify that they received their basic biblical education, practical training and dynamic inspiration from what is now Calvary Bible College and Theological Seminary and Dr. Walter L. Wilson, prime founder of KCBC. They rejoice in God's leading them to the school while they were yet in their teens and treasure the learning, the experiences and the firm foundation they gained.

EARLY LIFE AND ACADEMIC DEGREES

Geraldine Marquis was born March 26, 1925. She attended and graduated from the 8th grade in a one room school house, finishing her high school diploma at Washington Rural High School in Kansas City, Kansas. At the age of 18 she accepted the claims of Christ on her life in answer to Matthew 27:22. By 1945 she was teaching the Word of God.

Missions	Calvary Bible College (KCBC) 1948
Missions	Medical Missionary Institute 1949
B.A.	Calvary Bible College 1952
M.R.E.	Jackson College 1964
M.A.	Louisiana Baptist University 1994
Ph.D.	Louisiana Baptist University 1995

HONORARIA

L.H.D.	Jackson College 1965
LL.D.	Torrey Bible Institute 1986

Your Personal Study Notes

A study guide for *Search the Scriptures for Yourself* has been prepared by Stephen Rost, BA, MA, MDIV, STD and can be downloaded at www.21stcenturypress.com.